Unveiling Your Mask

FIND HEALING FROM REJECTION, JOURNEY INTO
SELF DISCOVERY AND WALK IN YOUR TRUE
IDENTITY

Shyann Owens

UNVEILING YOUR MASK

First edition. March 22, 2024.

Written by Shyann Owens.

Table of Contents

FOREWORD

In this present culture of mistaken identity, many individuals are living their lives in misaligned purpose, and outside the original plan God has for their life. As a result, they open themselves up to a world of confusion, hopelessness, unforgiveness, rejection and fear. Their identity becomes skewed and misaligned because they do not have a right relationship with Christ by knowing who he is, and our position in Him. It is In Him, that we have our true identity. This book is written for such a time as this, to help us align with the purpose and plan of God for this season and to get on the right path of walking in our true identity. Walking in our true identify breaks us free from the bondages, misalignments, and confusion of this world. God has placed value on each one of us and each one of us is an original in His eyes. Its time to line up with His original intent for us. The original will always hold value. Nevertheless, not My will, but Your will be done..

Laverne Pope

INTRODUCTION

My life is a testimony of the power and the deliverance of God's Word. As someone who has gotten to a crossroads of struggling with questions like, "Who am I?, Why am I here? Where do I belong"? etc., I understand the pain, confusion and frustration of not knowing your identity and purpose.

Like a soul adrift in a sea of confusion and turmoil, desperately seeking meaning and purpose. This was the reality for many of us before encountering the life-changing truth of our identity in Christ. For many people, the journey of walking in your true identity is a winding path, laced with challenges, doubts and uncertainties, as they are hooked in the web of identity crisis. In my previous book, I addressed this problem, sharing my personal stories of how I discovered my identity in Christ. I shared about my childhood experience, how my identity was suppressed from a tender age and how being quiet became my bondage. I did not know that my deliverance is tied to my confession.

I also had to deal with having a false identity, and how it affected my relationships. More hurtful was my experience being around some leaders who knew how much I needed help but couldn't help me because they had their own battles with rejection and identity crisis, too. My encounter with Jesus made me realize that a relationship with God is the ultimate, and other friendships or relationships come behind in the line. These relationships become better defined after I cultivated my relationship with Christ.

At some point, I depended on worldly things to define my identity. I was living the life I didn't want to live and becoming someone I didn't like. I was losing my integrity and authenticity. I became lost in cultures, thoughts and lifestyles that displeased God. I was in debt, because I was finding my identity through worldly possessions, only to lose everything. I began to nurse suicidal thoughts and making attempts. I was believing the lies of the devil that I was worthless and useless. Thank God for the Holy Spirit. The transforming work of the Holy Spirit renewed my mind with scriptures till my thoughts became influenced by the mind of Christ. His heart's desire became mine and His will became my will. This way, I began to detect and reject the lies of the devil.

The turning point for me was when I genuinely accepted Jesus Christ into my life and was baptized in the Holy Spirit in 2009. I felt starved and hungry; I needed to be satisfied. I developed discernment and could detect wrong teachings while listening to pastors preaching. God began to purge me, exposing me to prayers and revelations in deeper ways. Light came for me when I realized that God knows who I am; He knows me even before I was conceived. Not just that, He also created me with a purpose in mind. From that time, I decided that I would not let anyone profess what God has not said about my life and I will not go anywhere without God's permission.

When you discover your true identity, you become sensitive to what people say to you, the people you relate with and the places you go. To live in your true identity, you will need to discover how important these things are and walk rightly in them. I stopped living as a slave and became the heir that I am in Christ. Walking in your true identity is not first a journey of manifestation, but of healing and wholeness. It is a journey of constant and continuous deliverance as you strive to cultivate a living relationship with Christ.

The journey has been marked by twists and turns, triumphs and tribulations. It is a journey of revelations, of unearthing the buried treasures of my true identity hidden beneath layers of doubt and insecurity. After a series of uneasiness and several obstacles, I have come to full circle, I am back to my Maker, in total brokenness and surrender. For me, it is a new season, and I'm so glad and confident about my new journeys in Christ.

This book is an invitation to journey with me, as we explore how to live fully in the freedom of Christ. This is a call to receive the grace of God and the unwavering support of the Holy Spirit, as we press on in life and purpose. Soul ties are severed, doors are closed, and deliverance and wholeness are prevalent. But what does it mean to come full circle? It means embracing the fullness of who we are in Christ; no longer shackled by the chains of past hurts or insecurities but liberated to walk boldly in the truth of our identity as sons and daughters of the Most High.

Coming full circle meant stepping into a new season of my life; a season marked by restoration, renewal, and redemption. It meant reclaiming lost ground, reconciling broken relationships, and walking in the freedom that comes from knowing who I am in Christ. Walking in our true identity is not just about knowing who we are; it's about living out that truth in every aspect of our lives. It's about walking in wholeness and purpose, embracing our unique gifts and talents, and using them to glorify God and bless others. It's about being the hands and feet of Jesus in a broken and hurting world, sharing His love and compassion with those in need.

As you embark on this journey of walking in your true identity, hold fast to the promise of full circle. Be ready to embrace the truth that you are fearfully and wonderfully made, destined for a purpose far greater than you can imagine. And walk boldly in the freedom and authority that comes from knowing who you are in Christ.

CHAPTER 1

APPOINTED AND ANOINTED

"Before I formed you in the womb, I knew you; before you were born, I sanctified you; and I ordained you a prophet to the nations."

- Jeremiah 1:5

There was an awakening in me when I realized that God has defined and established my identity before I was conceived by my parents. He knew me before I was born. This realization was the beginning of my awakening and my journey in growth. I became more intentional about my life, what I think about my life, and what I say about what I can do. I became more Spirit-conscious and self-aware of who God made me to be. Generally, there has been an uprising about the desire to know one's identity.

Globally, there is an identity quest in the heart of everyone, irrespective of the nation, tribe and tongue. Every culture is quite particular in the subject of an individual's pursuit of discovering, knowing and understanding one's identity. There are several personality tests, vision boards, purpose assessment and many others, available for people to explore, as they quest to know who they are.

Your knowledge of who you are influences how you see yourself, which is often an outcome of your upbringing and early life experiences. It's possible you had a good upbringing and enjoyed the love and comfort of a healthy family and community life. It's also possible that the people you love said or did some things that made you develop self-doubt and low self-esteem. I used to be in your shoes, but our experiences may be different from one another.

The quest for identity is a profound journey that often defines our purpose, shapes our choices, and molds our character. Yet, for Christians, the pursuit of identity is beyond mere self-discovery; it is a transformational experience of knowing who we are in Christ. It is a journey of understanding our true identity as individuals, and how we are all woven into the fabric of God's divine plan.

Everyone is in pursuit of knowing who they are, what they look like and where they belong. Identity is a combination of many things, including experiences, exposure, memories, uniqueness, values, and relationships that create a sense of self. Knowing and understanding your identity in Christ gives you the revelation of your worth, purpose and how God sees you.

The answer to the identity question is in the Bible. The Bible says, "So God created mankind in his own image, in the image of God he created them; male and female he created them" (Genesis 1:27 NIV). Both males and females are created in God's image; this implies that they are meant to reflect and demonstrate some of the attributes of Godhood. While you can partake in personality tests and identity assessments, your true identity can only be found in Christ.

It's possible you are born again, you know you were forgiven, and you are heaven-bound, but you have no joy, peace and knowledge of how to live healthily and victoriously. It's possible you live in perpetual condemnation, and self-disdain. You will realize that when you're pursuing a goal, you feel a bit better because you thought that defines you a bit. However, by the time the task ends, you returned to your frustrated, miserable self. If you have ever felt like this, YOU ARE NOT ALONE!

Understanding True Identity in Christ

Generally, it is natural for you to seek your identity in external things. People look at their background, financial status, or even career to understand their identity. They spend time, resources and energy in the pursuit of their career. The job defines their lives, as it takes a major part of their time and focus. The truth is you can't find your true identity in external things. Identity stems from the inside, the heart, the source of all issues of life.

For a believer who has accepted Jesus Christ and has experienced the indwelling of God's Spirit, there is a change that happens from the inside, it occurs as a result of our mystical union with Christ. There is a consistent theme in the New Testament of the Bible, and this is the concept of being "in Christ". When we believed, we were translocated from the kingdom of darkness to the kingdom of light, where we dwell in Christ. Being in Christ is a union with Him, and it is beyond any label, title or identity we can ever think of. This union is transformative and prepares us for the final unveiling of our true identity as sons of God.

Paul, an apostle of Christ, who wrote most of the epistles of the New Testament, captures this reality in the Bible. He testified, declaring, "I have been crucified with Christ; it is no longer I who live, but Christ lives in me" (Galatians 2:20). As new creatures, our identity is no longer exclusive of our individuality, but an intimate union with Christ - He lives in us and we in Him.

Understanding our identity in Christ is to grasp the essence of our being as redeemed, beloved children of God. It is to acknowledge that our worth and value are not derived from worldly materials, money, accolades or achievements but from our status as heirs of God's kingdom. This foundational understanding makes the difference.

When God created humankind, He didn't mass produce them; He created, made and fashioned everyone in a very unique way. He created you with a purpose in mind and considered every detail of your life. He loves you with an everlasting love. Beyond loving you, He chose you! You may be wondering if God knows you. The Bible established that God knew us from the womb.

"For you created my inmost being you knit me together in my mother's womb. I praise you because I am fearfully and wonderfully made; your works are wonderful; I know that full well. My frame was not hidden from you when I was made in the secret place, when I was woven together in the depths of the earth. Your eyes saw my unformed body; all the days ordained for me were written in your book before one of them came to be" (Psalms 139:13-16 NIV).

Appointed and Anointed

God told Jeremiah, "before I formed you, I knew you". God knows you; He knows you before you were conceived. He knows your name before you were christened. He knows who you are and what He created you to become. He knows what you are capable of, and how strong you are. Before you were born, you have carried an ordination and an anointing. Your ordination and anointing are not from a theological seminary or the laying on of hands. They are from God, He appointed and anointed you before your parents gave birth to you.

You need to understand that you don't need to seek validation from people. You don't need people's approval to be who you are meant to be. God knows who you are, and He has given you gifts and graces to distinguish you from others. You are not another being, you are a special person! You are called and chosen. You are appointed and anointed! Your appointment predates your conception. Your ordination predates your birth. When you realize this, God's anointing and power will come alive in you! Hallelujah!

Just as Jeremiah's calling transcended human agency, yours is also rooted in God's preordained plan. From the very inception of his existence, Jeremiah was appointed for a specific purpose—to be a mouthpiece for God, proclaiming truth to the nations. You were chosen for a specific purpose and assignment. This divine appointment underscores the truth that your identities are not haphazard or accidental but intricately designed by the Creator Himself.

Moreover, Jeremiah's anointing symbolizes the empowering presence of God's Spirit in fulfilling his prophetic mandate. Just as oil was ceremonially poured upon prophets, priests, and kings in the Old Testament as a sign of God's equipping and empowering, Jeremiah was anointed with a divine commission to speak forth God's words with authority and conviction.

Dear reader, you are not just on earth as a result of the conception, or misconception, of your parents. You are specially created for a specific purpose, with divine gifts and unique graces. Your identity is deeply rooted in who God ordained you to be, not in what the society defines you to be. People may call you broken, but God made you whole. People may call you forsaken, but God called you married. People may say you are ugly, but God who created you said you are wonderfully and beautifully created!

Shaping Worth and Identity

The revelation of Jeremiah's appointment and anointing serves as a paradigm for understanding your worth and identity in Christ. Like Jeremiah, you are not mere products of chance or circumstance; you are purposefully crafted vessels in the hands of a sovereign God. Your intrinsic value is not based upon external validation or societal standards but is rooted in your identity as beloved children of God.

Imagine the confidence, peace and honor of being a son or daughter to the president of your country. Now consider the confidence, peace, beauty, grace and glamour of being a child of God, a chosen prince and princess of the Great Monarch of Heaven. This is who you are! Understanding your appointment and anointing in Christ shapes your sense of worth by affirming your significance in God's redemptive plan. It instills within you a profound sense of purpose and belonging, enabling you to embrace your true identity with confidence and assurance.

As recipients of God's grace and mercy, you are called to walk in the fullness of our identity, knowing that you have been uniquely appointed and anointed for divine purposes. Whatever anyone or the devil tells you does not matter; the One who made you has spoken! Whose report will you believe?

Your confidence and worth should come from knowing God's Word, knowing what God said concerning you. I know you are used to what people call you, but it's time to start knowing what God calls you! It's time to start responding to the voice and words of God. You need to start seeing yourself the way God sees you! He doesn't call you by your past or circumstances; He calls you by the name of who He made you to be!

Discovering Purpose and Calling

Central to embracing your true identity in Christ is the pursuit of discovering your unique purpose and calling. Just as Jeremiah was ordained as a prophet to the nations, you have been endowed with specific gifts, talents, and passions designed to advance God's kingdom agenda. This journey of discovery involves seeking God's guidance, discerning His voice, and aligning your life with His will.

Sometimes, inability to know who you are prevents you from knowing and fulfilling your purpose and calling. Sometimes you may feel out of place, and you start cultivating questions about who you are and why you are. Truth is, you are not alone. God wants you to know who you are and fulfilling your purpose. He is very much interested in you knowing, as much you are interested.

The fear of change also keeps people from recognizing and realizing who they are. They are afraid of what people will say when they make the decision to change. They don't want to lose their sense of belonging and the approval of others around them. So, they remain in their shell. One thing really matters, and that's you and your decision. At the end, they have nothing to lose if you change or not. You wouldn't want to live in the regret of not knowing and fulfilling your purpose. This fear of changing gets stronger when you become accustomed to living in a particular way for a long time.

Also, the fear of external influences like the society, family members and friends can make you want to confirm to some identities or live to certain expectations. You may find yourself confused or in self-doubt. Whatever circumstances you are in, don't forget that knowing your true identity and living purposefully make the journey of life interesting and adventurous. Purpose makes life worth living. Knowing who you are is a lifelong journey and not just a one-time thing. Take your time, make mistakes, get up, heal and become whole in the process. What matters is that you are able to stay true to who you are and making progress.

Through prayer, meditation on Scripture, and seeking wise counsel, you can uncover God's purposes for your life. It is a journey marked by surrender, obedience, and trust, as you yield your ambitions and aspirations to God's sovereign direction. As you align your hearts with God's purposes, His anointing empowers you to fulfill your divine destiny and make a significant impact in the world around you.

Empowered by His Anointing

The anointing of God's Spirit is not merely a symbolic gesture but a tangible empowerment that enables you to walk in obedience and effectiveness. Just as the disciples were filled with the Holy Spirit at Pentecost, you too are a recipient of God's empowering presence. This anointing equips you with spiritual gifts, divine wisdom, and supernatural power to fulfill the callings and assignments God has entrusted to you.

Moreover, the anointing serves as a catalyst for transformation, both within you and through you. It enables you to overcome obstacles, conquer challenges, and impact lives for the glory of God. As vessels of His anointing, you are called to be conduits of His love, mercy, and grace, shining as beacons of hope in a world shrouded in darkness.

In God's redemptive plan, understanding your appointment and anointing in Christ is paramount. It is a journey of self-discovery rooted in the eternal truth of our identity as beloved children of God. Just as Jeremiah was appointed and anointed for a divine purpose, so too are you called to embrace your true identity and walk in the fullness of your calling.

As you surrender your lives to God's sovereign will, He empowers you with His anointing, enabling you to fulfill your divine destiny and make a lasting impact in the world around us. May you, like Jeremiah, boldly proclaim God's truth, embody His love, and walk in the fullness of your identity as an appointed and anointed child of the Most High.

CHAPTER 2

THE QUEST BEGINS

"You will seek me and find me when you seek me with all your heart" - Jeremiah 29:13

Welcome! I am glad you have chosen to go on this journey to walk in your true identity. I once made this momentous decision. It is a declaration of courage, curiosity, and commitment to uncovering the depths of your being. I am genuinely glad that you have chosen to embark on this quest, for it is a journey that holds the potential to transform your life in profound and meaningful ways.

I am glad you've made the decision to be true to who you are, for it is a decision that will set you on a path of endless possibilities and infinite potential. Embrace this journey with courage, curiosity, and an open heart, and know that with each step you take, you are moving closer to becoming the person you were always meant to be.

In choosing to walk in the light of who you are, you are stepping into a realm of infinite possibilities. This is a realm where the boundaries of self-imposed limitations are dissolved, and the horizon stretches out before you. You are yielding to the call to explore, to grow, and to become. It is a journey where every experience, encounter, and revelation serves as a stepping stone towards realizing your fullest potential.

In this journey, you will need to open yourself to new experiences. As you navigate the twists and turns of this journey, I encourage you to approach each moment with an open heart and an open mind. Embrace the uncertainties, the challenges, and the moments of discomfort, for it is in these moments that the seeds of growth are sown. Allow yourself to explore every avenue, to question every assumption, and to challenge every belief, for it is through this process of exploration that you will uncover the hidden treasures of your true self.

The Bible says, "You will seek me and find me when you seek me with all your heart". This quest requires that you seek God with all your heart. Pursue God wholeheartedly in your quest for identity. Sincerity and earnestness in seeking God are important, as He assures that those who seek Him diligently will find Him. God responds to genuine seekers. He that seeks Him diligently will find Him.

Our true identity can only be found in Him. Over the years, our true identity is locked up in wrong beliefs, assumptions and perspectives. We have believed wrong things people said about us and accepted the boxes of limitations placed on our potentials. Of course, this journey is not one where we cast blames. We are here to take responsibility for the direction of our lives. We are on this quest to get out of the box.

Remember that walking in your true identity is not a destination but a continuous journey; it is a journey of becoming. It is a journey where you accept who you are, love who you are and empower yourself in the light of who you are. The revelation of your true identity is empowering, and capable of shifting you into a new season. This is a quest where you learn to embrace every aspect of who you are with compassion and grace. It is a journey of identity-expression, where you learn to honor your unique gifts, talents, and passions, and to share them with the world in meaningful and authentic ways.

So, as you set out on this quest, know that you are not alone. You are surrounded by a community of fellow travelers. They are those who have walked this path before you, those who walk alongside you and there are those you will also take on this journey, after you have mastered the process. As you journey, draw strength from their wisdom, their encouragement, and their support, and know that together, you can navigate the complexities of this journey and emerge stronger, wiser, and more fully alive.

While the human experience is a vast expanse, there is a particular quest that is beyond migration or geographical boundaries. It is beyond the temporal constraints of time, space and matter. It is a journey of earthly significance and eternal consequence. As you embark on this journey, you will unearth the depths of your being, and uncover the true essence of your identity. Like explorers charting uncharted territories, you need your sense of anticipation, curiosity, and longing. This is the journey of the soul, the quest to find your true identity in Christ.

Setting Out on the Journey

"Trust in the Lord with all your heart and lean not on your own understanding; in all your ways submit to him, and he will make your paths straight." (Proverbs 3:5-6). There is a need to trust God with all your heart; relying on His guidance and surrendering to His will as you set out on the journey. Do not rely on your own understanding or ideas, but on God's wisdom.

Every journey begins with a single step, a decision to embark on an adventure into the unknown. Similarly, the identity quest commences with a moment of introspection, a recognition of the need to go deeper into the recesses of your heart and mind, trusting and relying on God's wisdom alone. It is a journey fueled by a desire for authenticity, a yearning to peel back the layers of societal expectations, personal insecurities, and cultural conditioning to reveal the true self beneath.

Societal expectations have done a great damage to many people's identities. It is possible you keep hearing the voices of those expectations, questioning why you need to make this decision, why you think about the right step, why you think it is time, how will it happen, what if you don't discover what you seek, the "what ifs"... I want you to understand that you are more than what others think, say or want of you. Your parents might want you to stay with them, as long as you don't grow to leave them, they are comfortable. Your friends might want to use peer pressure to keep you in locked up in bad habits. You are more than what the society expects of you. Don't allow the societal box to keep you from going on this quest.

Every moment and season of your life are regulated by your decisions. Everything you do submits to the power of your decision. The time you sleep, the time you get out of bed, or whether to stay in bed, are part of the decisions you make daily. The food you eat, the cloth you wear, how to style them, to study or work, to build or break, are subject to your decision. Whether it is to dye your hair or cut it, it's also subjective to the decision you make. In fact, part of the decisions you've made today is to read this book. You could have chosen not to, or opt to spend some time on Facebook or Instagram.

The decisions you make affect everything you do. You either make your decisions or they are made for you. Your decisions can be influenced by the decisions of those around you. Everything you do in life is driven by the decision you make. We live with the consequence of a decision we take or did not take. The decisions you make affect others, and the decisions of people around you affect you. Someone might see you reading this book and develop interests in this quest as well. Realizing the power of decisions, you need to begin to think of prioritizing yourself and the decisions you make. You might need to take a moment to reflect your life and the decisions you've taken over the years. You are either a victim or a beneficiary of your decisions and that of others.

As you set out, you are confronted with a myriad of questions, doubts, and uncertainties. Who am I? What is my purpose? Where do I belong? These questions serve as compass points guiding you on our quest, urging you to seek answers beyond the surface level of existence. It is by questioning that we get answers, light and direction.

The Power of Walking in your True Identity

Why is this pursuit crucial? What compels us to embark on this journey of introspection and examination? It is a recognition that true happiness and contentment cannot be found in external possessions or fleeting pleasures but in the depths of our own souls, in the heart of who God made us to be. As Christians, we are called to live out our faith, not as a mere set of beliefs or doctrines, but as a transformative reality that permeates every aspect of our lives. To truly understand who we are in Christ is to embrace the fullness of our identity as beloved children of God, redeemed and restored by His grace.

Furthermore, walking in your true identity is crucial because it empowers us to live authentically and purposefully. One of the significant expressions of who we are as Christians is that we are the "light of the world". This is something that is worthy of reflection. Here is what the Bible says about this, "Ye are the light of the world. A city that is set on a hill cannot be hid. Neither do men light a candle, and put it under a bushel, but on a candlestick; and it giveth light unto all that are in the house. Let your light so shine before men, that they may see your good works, and glorify your Father which is in heaven." (Matthew 5:14-16 KJV).

I love the New International Version (NIV). It says, "You are the light of the world. A town built on a hill cannot be hidden. Neither do people light a lamp a nd put it under a bowl. Instead, they put it on its stand, and it gives light to everyone in the house. In the same way, let your light shine before others, that they may see your good deeds and glorify your Father in heaven."

You are a light, and you are not meant to be hidden. You have stayed hidden for too long. You have hidden under fears, doubt, frustration, abuse, pain, unforgiveness, lies and trauma for too long. That's not who you are! You are not a wonder that is meant to be hidden. You are a force, a solution, a source of hope and comfort to the world. Whatever the bowl that you or others have used to cover your light, it is time to remove it. This is your season!

It's time to begin to peel back the layers of societal expectations and cultural conditioning, so that you can be liberated from the shackles of conformity and empowered to embrace your unique gifts, talents, and passions. This authenticity enables you to live with integrity, confidence, and conviction, shining as beacons of light in a world shrouded in darkness.

There is a great power in walking in the light of who you are, and it is transformational. This power transcends mere self-awareness and leads to profound personal growth and development. To discover this power, you must deal with your fears, insecurities, and limitations. In this quest, you find the courage to confront these inner demons and emerge stronger, wiser, and more resilient.

Moreover, this authentic walk fosters a deeper understanding of your true worth and value as individuals created in the image of God. It is a journey of self-acceptance and self-love, a recognition that you are fearfully and wonderfully made, endowed with infinite worth and significance in the eyes of your Creator. This realization empowers you to embrace your flaws and imperfections, knowing that you are loved unconditionally by the One who formed you in His image.

Furthermore, walking in your true identity cultivates a deeper intimacy with God as you come to understand who you are in Christ. It is a journey of spiritual awakening, a recognition that your truest self is found in union with Christ, our Savior and Lord. As you align your life with God's purposes and plans, you experience a profound sense of peace, joy, and fulfillment that transcend earthly desires and ambitions.

CHAPTER 3

UNVEILING YOUR MASK

"You were taught, with regard to your former way of life, to put off your old self, which is being corrupted by its deceitful desires; to be made new in the attitude of your minds; and to put on the new self, created to be like God in true righteousness and holiness." - Ephesians 4:22-24

In your search for acceptance and purpose, you may often adopt false identities, roles, and personas that deviate from your true self to fit in or stand out. You may become people-pleasers, sacrificing your own needs and desires to gain the approval of others. You may become overachievers, striving relentlessly for success and recognition at the expense of your well-being. You may become chameleons, adapting your personalities and behaviors to conform to different social contexts and expectations.

Yet, the more you cling to these false identities, the further you stray from your true self, losing sight of the unique beauty and potential that resides within you. You become trapped in a cycle of self-deception, constantly seeking validation and affirmation from external sources rather than finding fulfillment from within. You may experience moments of fleeting satisfaction or temporary acclaim, but deep down, you know that you are living a lie, which ultimately robs you of joy, authenticity, and genuine connection.

The above passage emphasizes the need to discard the old self, which is characterized by deceitful desires, and embrace the new self, created in righteousness and holiness. There is a need for you to let go of the false identities of your old self and embrace their true identity in Christ.

Uncovering the Truth Behind the Facades

2 Corinthians 5:17 - "Therefore, if anyone is in Christ, the new creation has come: The old has gone, the new is here!" Note that this scripture emphasizes the transformational power of being in Christ. When you identify with Christ in salvation and identity, you become a new creation, as your

old identities are gone. Your new life is now in Christ. Anything outside of Christ is not allowed in your life.

Unveiling your masks and embracing your authentic self begins with a willingness to confront the truth; the truth about who you are, what you value, and what truly matters to you. It requires courage to peel back the layers of deception and self-denial, to acknowledge your fears, insecurities, and vulnerabilities without judgment or shame.

To uncover the truth behind the facades, you must be willing to engage in introspection and self-reflection. You must examine the motives behind your actions, the beliefs that shape your perceptions, and the masks that obscure your true self. You must confront the voices of doubt and self-criticism that whisper lies of unworthiness and inadequacy, replacing them with truths of love, acceptance, and belonging.

Moreover, you must be willing to seek guidance and support from trusted mentors, counselors, or spiritual advisors who can provide insight and perspective as you walk in your true identity. They can help you identify patterns of behavior, thought, and emotion that may be contributing to your false identity and offer tools and techniques for breaking free from their grip.

Unmasking

People are often masked. These masks, though they may serve as shields against judgment and rejection, ultimately imprison you in a web of deception, preventing you from experiencing the freedom and authenticity you crave. Beneath these facades lies a deeper truth; a truth yearning to be unveiled and embraced. Behind the mask of perfection lies the vulnerability of imperfection, the beauty of our flaws, and the authenticity of our struggles. Behind the mask of success lies the humility of failure, the acknowledgment of our limitations, and the acceptance of our humanity. Behind the mask of popularity lies the solitude of authenticity; the freedom to be true to ourselves and to forge genuine connections with others based on honesty and vulnerability.

Consider and ponder this question: How many versions of you are there? It's a question worth pondering, for many people wear different masks and play different roles depending on the situation or environment they find themselves. Are you a different person at work than who you are at home? Are you a different person behind the wheel of your car than you are when speaking to your parents? Do you play one part at church and another part with friends during the week or on weekends? Do you hide parts of yourself or change the way you present yourself based on circumstances?

The truth is, we all engage in a degree of adaptation to fit our situations. It's natural to adjust our behavior, mannerisms, and even speech depending on the situation we find ourselves in. Just as we wouldn't wear the same clothes to a formal event as we would to a casual gathering, we tailor our behavior to suit the social norms and expectations of each setting. However, these adaptations become more extreme when we find ourselves morphing into entirely different personas depending on the circumstance, it can be a cause for concern.

From an early age, we are taught to conform to societal expectations and norms, molding ourselves into shapes deemed acceptable by the world around us. We wear masks of perfection, striving to project an image of flawlessness and invincibility to shield ourselves from criticism and ridicule. We wear masks of success, measuring our worth by external achievements and accolades rather than intrinsic value. We wear masks of popularity, seeking validation and approval from others at the expense of our true desires and convictions.

For many people, wearing masks to fit into different situations is a mere survival mechanism, and this is deeply rooted in their desire for social acceptance and belonging. We learn from an early age that certain behaviors are rewarded, and others are punished, and we adapt accordingly to navigate the complexities of our interactions with people. There is a problem when you become adaptable to the point that you are no longer authentic. Don't lose your authenticity in an attempt to fit into friendship circles, places, and society. When you hide parts of yourself or suppress your true emotions to fit in or avoid conflict, you sacrifice your integrity and betray your innermost values and beliefs.

Moreover, constantly shifting between different personas can be exhausting and disorienting. It can leave you feeling fragmented and disconnected from your true self, unsure of who you are beneath the layers of social conditioning and adaptation. The story of the Samaritan woman at the well illustrates this so well. In the Gospel of John, you will find

Jesus's encounter with a woman at the well. She comes to draw water from the well in the heat of the day; a time when most women would avoid the scorching sun and gather water in the coolness of the morning or evening.

At first, the Samaritan woman appears to be simply going about her daily routine, fetching water for her household. But as the passage unfolds, we begin to see that she is wearing more than just the mask of a dutiful housewife; she is hiding behind layers of shame, guilt, and societal rejection. She has had five husbands and even the man at home isn't married to her. As Jesus engaged her in conversation, he gently peeled back these layers, revealing the woman's true self. The Bible says,

"He told her, Go, call your husband and come back." "I have no husband," she replied. Jesus said to her, "You are right when you say you have no husband. The fact is, you have had five husbands, and the man you now have is not your husband. What you have just said is quite true." "Sir," the woman said, "I can see that you are a prophet." (John 4:16-19 NIV)

With grace, compassion, and understanding, Jesus acknowledged her past mistakes and shortcomings, her multiple marriages, and her current relationship outside of wedlock. In this moment of vulnerability and authenticity, the Samaritan woman experiences a profound transformation. She recognizes Jesus as more than just a stranger at the well; He is the Messiah, the One who sees her for who she truly is and loves her unconditionally. The instant transformation to recognizing Him ignited a deep sense of worship in her. She immediately brought up a long unanswered question about her worship of God.

This moment of revelation is what you need to come out of your shell. You need to recognize Him, so you can come as you are. You need to know that He is not waiting to condemn you. He is looking forward to meeting, washing, and dressing you. He wants to show you how much He loved you, while you were yet sinner. He wants to hold you by the hand in your journey towards authenticity. It's time for you to come to the well to meet your Savior; the One who loves your soul.

In response, the Samaritan Woman left her water jar behind and rushed back to her village, eager to share her encounter with the One who knows her fully and yet loves her completely. She left the water jar, a similitude of her masks. She became the first evangelist of Christ. She was masking up, hiding behind sexual and marital relationships to find a sense of being. She knew something was wrong with her and looked forward to the coming of the Messiah. The Bible says, "The woman said, "I know that Messiah" (called Christ) "is coming. When he comes, he will explain everything to us." (John 4:25 NIV). She looked forward to seeing Him, to learning from Him.

Do you like this woman, desiring to see Jesus, looking forward to learning and hearing from Him about everything? Jesus is there with you. You can embrace His presence. Just believe. You will feel His warmth, love, and kindness. Talk to Him. Don't hold back your tears. Take away those masks, one after the other, and give them to Him. Take away the bowls that you have covered your light.

The story of the Samaritan woman illustrates the danger of masking up and of hiding behind layers of shame, guilt, and societal expectations. It reminds us that true freedom and fulfillment can only be found in authenticity and vulnerability. It shows us that it is only when we allow ourselves to be seen and known for who we truly are that we can experience genuine connection and belonging.

Moreover, the Samaritan woman's encounter with Jesus challenges us to rethink our assumptions and judgments about others. Just as Jesus saw beyond the Samaritan woman's social status and past mistakes to her true worth and potential, so too are we called to see beyond the masks that others wear and to recognize their inherent dignity and value as children of God.

In a world that often encourages us to hide our true selves behind masks of perfection, success, or conformity, the story of the Samaritan woman serves as a powerful reminder that we can still find identity and purpose in Christ. Jesus invites you to lay down your masks and embrace your true self; He invites you to come to the well, as you are, and encounter the One who knows you fully and loves you completely.

So how do you navigate this delicate balance between adapting to fit the context and remaining true to yourself? It starts with self-awareness and introspection. You must take the time to examine your motivations and behaviors, to identify the masks you wear and the roles you play, and to discern whether they align with your authentic self.

From there, you can begin the process of integration, aligning the disparate parts of yourself with your core values and beliefs. This may involve setting boundaries, asserting your true feelings and opinions, and challenging the societal norms and expectations that constrain you. It also requires vulnerability and courage; the willingness to be seen and accepted for who you truly are, flaws and all. It means embracing your authenticity and embracing the messy, imperfect, beautifully human self that you are.

In the end, the goal is not to eliminate all versions of ourselves, but to integrate them into a cohesive whole; a whole that is authentic, genuine, and true to who we are at our core. By doing so, we can live with integrity, authenticity, and purpose, and engage in human interaction with grace, compassion, and authenticity.

Shedding the Masks to Embrace Authenticity

To walk in your true identity, you need to shed the masks you wear and embrace your authentic self. This is not a one-time event but an ongoing process. It is a journey of growth, healing, and transformation. It requires vulnerability to let go of the safety and security of your false identity, and step into the unknown territory of authenticity. It requires humility to acknowledge your imperfections and limitations and embrace them as integral parts of who you are. It requires courage to stand firm in your convictions, values, and beliefs, even in the face of opposition or rejection.

Yet, as you shed the masks, embrace and walk in your authentic self, you will experience a profound sense of liberation and empowerment. You will discover a newfound freedom to express yourself fully and authentically, unencumbered by the expectations and judgments of others. You will cultivate deeper connections and relationships based on mutual respect, trust, and understanding. You will find joy, fulfillment, and purpose in aligning your life with your true self and living in harmony with your values and passions.

CHAPTER 4

FREEDOM FROM OFFENCE

"Get rid of all bitterness, rage and anger, brawling and slander, along with every form of malice. Be kind and compassionate to one another, forgiving each other, just as in Christ God forgave you." - Ephesians 4:31-32

True freedom from offense starts with genuine forgiveness. Being free from something's lordship or rule is what we all understand freedom to mean. This suggests that the offense itself has the power to subjugate people and imprison them (bring them under a rule) for extended periods, which would eventually cause resentment/bitterness. Let us first define what an offense is. Offense, in its simplest form, is the feeling of resentment, anger, or hurt caused by a perceived slight or wrongdoing. It manifests in various contexts, from personal interactions to societal dynamics, and can have profound implications for individuals and communities alike.

The Biblical meaning of offense is an injury or wrong done to one (1 Samuel 25:31; Romans 5:15). It can also mean a stumbling block or cause of temptation (Isaiah 8:14; Matthew 16:23; 18:7). Greek standalone, properly that at which one stumble or takes offense. The "offense of the cross" (Galatians 5:11) is the offense the Jews took at the teaching that salvation was by the crucified One and by him alone. Salvation by the cross was a stumbling block to their national pride.

In the journey of walking our true identity, one of the greatest obstacles we may encounter is the burden of offense. This can mask and hinder genuine friendships and relationships but also impair our ability but also impair our ability to trust and submit to true authority figures. I also found myself ensnared by the shackles of a false identity, which cast a shadow over my interactions and perceptions.

Growing up with trust issues stemming from a strained relationship with my natural father, I struggled to trust and submit to those in positions of authority. This lack of trust and submission was not only detrimental to my personal growth but also hindered my ability to receive help from those who genuinely sought to assist me. Offense, fueled by a distorted sense of self-esteem, prevented me from embracing the guidance and support offered by others.

As I shared previously, one of the most painful experiences I encountered was the betrayal of trust by leaders who purported to offer assistance but instead exploited my vulnerability for their gain. Their deception left me offended, questioning my faith and feeling disillusioned with those who claimed to represent God. It was a harsh reminder of the prevalence of deception in the world and the importance of seeking discernment through the guidance of the Holy Spirit.

The Scriptures remind us that the heart of man is prone to offense, and only God can judge the true state and intentions of the heart. As you interact with others, you must recognize the inherent flaws and imperfections of humanity, avoiding undue expectations or misplaced trust. Instead, approach your relationships with others with a discerning spirit, allowing room for grace and forgiveness.

While the offense may sting, I am grateful for the lessons I learned through these experiences. They served as catalysts for my growth, leading me to prioritize my relationship with God above all else. In the journey to freedom from offense, you must remember that your ultimate relationship is with God through Jesus Christ. All other relationships and friendships pale in comparison to the depth of intimacy we can experience with our Creator.

By examining the different interpretations of what constitutes an offense, I also hope to dispel the myth that only our "enemies" commit an offense. The fact that it occurs from persons we least anticipate it from makes it a true offense. Most of the time, our pastors, trustworthy uncles, parents, siblings, Christian sisters and brothers, friends, spouses, or romantic partners are the ones who commit offenses against us. Although no one prays to commit offenses, they (humans) inevitably do!

The Bible recognizes the existence of offense and offers guidance on dealing with its intricacies in a kind and wise manner. Scripture contains numerous verses that address this issue. One of Jesus' teachings was on the subject of offense. In His teachings, Jesus admits that sins will inevitably occur in the world. While acknowledging that there are many potentials for offense to occur in human interactions, He also provides a serious caution against offending other people.

The Bible says, "Woe unto the world because of offenses! for it must need to be that offense come; but woe to that man by whom the offense cometh!" (Matthew 18:7). The word skandalon, translated as "offenses" or "offense," is used by Jesus three times in this verse. Skandalon is the trigger of a trap on which bait is placed. When an animal touches the trigger to eat the bait, the trap springs shut, and the animal is caught. When used in a moral context, skandalon indicates the enticement to conduct that will ruin the person in question. This verse underscores the importance of personal accountability and the need for conscientious conduct in our relationships.

The Bible says, "If it is possible, as much as lieth in you, live peaceably with all men". I would have appreciated it if we could have broken out the meaning of "if possible" in this passage and started addressing "you" as a believer rather than everyone else. It is your responsibility to work toward and make it feasible for all men to live in harmony and without offense. (Romans 12:18 KJV)

There is a need to be completely aware that there are forms of offense. It might be done purposefully or accidentally. You would undoubtedly want to know how an offense can occur accidentally. There are instances where someone feels insulted, yet the person who offended—the one who stumbled—then says they were unaware that the offense had even occurred. The important thing to remember is that an act might still be considered an offense even if it was done accidentally. It continues to be an offense if the person receiving the action suffers harm.

Establishing the fact that offenses will come, what needs to be done to get freedom from offense? Freedom from offense is not merely a lofty ideal but a tangible expression of the transformative power of grace and love. Grounded in biblical principles of forgiveness, reconciliation, and peacemaking, it serves as a beacon of hope in a world rife with division and discord. As you strive to embody the teachings of Scripture, may you be an agent of reconciliation and healing, extending God's boundless love and mercy to a hurting world.

Through the lens of Scripture, the call to freedom from offense resonates as a timeless imperative, inviting believers to embrace the transformative power of forgiveness, love, and reconciliation. In pursuing this noble ideal, may hearts be softened, relationships restored, and communities enriched by the enduring legacy of grace and compassion.

Freedom can be achieved when someone strongly revolts against an authority (stronghold) and fights till it is s granted. Sometimes, freedom needs to be fought for. The first way to be free from offense is to guide against offense strongly. The Bible clearly states, "for the weapons of our warfare are not carnal, but mighty through God to the pulling down of strong holds" (2 Corinthians 10:4 KJV).

As I said earlier, being under the control of offense is synonymous with being under the control of a stronghold that needs to be pulled down. One needs to guard against offense so as not to find oneself stuck under the control of such a stronghold. Assuredly, once one is caught in the web of offense, it holds one down strongly, and one would need some intentional act to be free from it. Why not guard against it instead of being caught in its web?

Guarding Against Offense

While pursuing freedom from offense is commendable, believers are also called to exercise discernment and wisdom in their interactions with others. Proverbs, with its practical wisdom, offers timeless insights into the importance of guarding one's heart against the snares of offense. The Bible says, "The discretion of a man makes him slow to anger, and his glory is to overlook a transgression." Proverbs 19:11. This proverb shows the value of discretion and discernment in navigating interpersonal dynamics. By exercising restraint and overlooking minor offenses, individuals demonstrate wisdom and maturity, preserving relationships and fostering a spirit of unity and goodwill.

Another way to freedom from offense is Pursuing Peace. Pursuing peace and reconciliation lies at the heart of biblical teachings on freedom from offense. Jesus, in His Sermon on the Mount, "Blessed are the peacemakers, for they shall be called sons of God," (Matthew 5:9) extols the virtues of peacemaking and offers practical guidance on resolving conflicts and restoring broken relationships. Also, in Hebrews 12:14 KJV, the Bible says, "Follow peace with all men, and holiness, without which no man shall see the

Lord:" "Follow" used in this verse of the scripture can also be interchanged with the word "pursue". You need to make a conscious and intentional effort to ensure you live in peace with yourself and others.

Peacemaking entails active engagement in the resolution of conflicts and the promotion of harmony and understanding. It requires humility, empathy, and a willingness to bridge divides and seek common ground. By embodying the principles of peacemaking, believers reflect the character of God and participate in the ongoing work of reconciliation in a fractured world. It requires that you look above all odds of age, gender, position, etc., to break free from the stronghold of offense.

We can pursue peace through wisdom in communication. The book of Proverbs provides valuable guidance on communication, stating, "A gentle answer turns away wrath, but a harsh word stirs up anger." Proverbs 15:1 (NIV). This principle encourages believers to communicate with wisdom and humility, avoiding unnecessary offense. James 3:2 (NIV) highlights the challenge of controlling the tongue: "We all stumble in many ways. Anyone who is never at fault in what they say is perfect, able to keep their whole body in check." This verse emphasizes the ongoing effort required to speak with wisdom and avoid offending.

Also, as believers, we can break through offense through Love. Love is the pinnacle of Christian virtues, guiding believers in their interactions with others and serving as a catalyst for reconciliation and unity. The apostle Paul's exhortation in 1 Corinthians provides profound insights into the transformative nature of love in overcoming offense. 1 Corinthians 13:4-7

"Love suffers long and is kind; love does not envy; love does not parade itself, is not puffed up; does not behave rudely, does not seek its own, is not provoked, thinks no evil; does not rejoice in iniquity, but rejoices in the truth; bears all things, believes all things, hopes all things, endures all things."

In these verses, Paul delineates the attributes of love, highlighting its enduring nature and its capacity to transcend petty grievances and offenses. Love fosters empathy, compassion, and humility, fostering an environment conducive to reconciliation and healing. By embodying the essence of love in their interactions, believers cultivate a spirit of forbearance and understanding, mitigating the potential for offense to disrupt relationships.

CHAPTER 5

WALKING IN FORGIVENESS

"Bear with each other and forgive one another if any of you has a grievance against someone. Forgive as the Lord forgave you." - Colossians 3:13 (NIV)

One of the significant things that happened to me was God forgiving me, and I forgave myself and others who wronged me. From our previous chapter, we reached a baseline for what offense is. In this chapter, we will see together the high calling of "walking" in forgiveness as one of the ways to walk in your true identity. Unforgiveness can mask you, and hold you in its shackles, preventing you from walking in your authentic self. Authenticity requires that you let go of unforgiveness. Walking in forgiveness is a continuous process; it's not a one-time thing. It's a matter that needs consistent practice. Little wonder when Peter, one of the disciples of Jesus, asked him (Jesus) how many times should a man forgive? Simply put, does forgiveness have a limit? Let's investigate it together.

Forgiveness Has No Limit

When Peter asked Jesus how often we should forgive those who offend us, Jesus' response was seventy times seven (Matthew 18:21-22 NKJV). Jesus did not only teach forgiveness, he offers forgiveness to us his children, and also to those who are lost, and he wants us to do the same. (1 John 1:9; Acts 2:38-39; Ephesians 1:7). He spoke about forgiveness several times and even incorporated it into the Lord's prayer, which is the prayer He modeled for His disciples (Matthew 6:12 NKJV).

Jesus did not state there is a 490-time limit. He was demonstrating that there is no upper limit to forgiveness. In the Bible, the number seventy-seven stands for wholeness, perfection, and fulfillment. To put it another way, Jesus asks us to forgive others fully. As I mentioned earlier, God has given us the ability to accomplish this through the power of the Holy Spirit's indwelling.

What is forgiveness? Forgiveness means to send away, release, and remit. Some profound quotes: "To forgive is to set a prisoner free and discover that the prisoner was you" (Lewis B. Smeded).

From the parable of the unmerciful servant, Jesus taught what it means to forgive. Simply put, forgiveness is to show mercy. Looking away from someone's offense and its punishments. The parable of the unmerciful servant, as Jesus taught, found in Matthew 18:21-35, tells the story of a servant who owed a huge debt to his master. When he couldn't repay, the master forgave him. However, the same servant refused to let go of a smaller debt owed to him by a fellow servant. The master, upon hearing this, revoked his forgiveness and punished him. This parable teaches the importance of forgiveness and mercy towards others, reflecting on God's forgiveness towards humanity. From this parable, can we agree that forgiveness means letting go? Yes, to forgive is to let go. Letting go of all the pains, the hurts, the anger, the bitterness, vexation, and so on. All of these can lead to anxiety, depression, high blood pressure, vascular resistance, a weakened immune system, and other conditions, which can also be poisonous to the spirit and one's state of mind and health. The ability to walk in forgiveness lessens this health issue.

Living in forgiveness can be so difficult. It can be among the more challenging things for a believer to undertake. It's normal to harbor grudges against someone for their transgression or to want them to pay for it. We all act wrongfully toward others and in ways that lead us to believe that we are flawed. Forgiveness is an act of obedience, not a sentiment. It is a command. In the Bible, forgiveness is not merely a suggestion but a commandment. Colossians 3:13 (NIV), says, "Bear with each other and forgive one another if any of you has a grievance against someone. Forgive as the Lord forgave you." This verse emphasizes the importance of forgiveness and reminds us of the model of forgiveness set by God himself it also emphasizes the qualities of "compassion, kindness, lowliness, meekness, and patience.

"Let all bitterness and wrath and anger and clamor and slander be put away from you, with all malice, and be kind to one another, tenderhearted, forgiving one another, as God in Christ forgave you." (Ephesians 4:31-32). It doesn't matter how you feel about forgiveness. You might never have the desire to walk in forgiveness. Walking in forgiveness is a decision to obey that which is based on your will rather than your feelings. Walking in forgiveness is a decision we make that affects every aspect of our lives.

Forgiveness toward others keeps our hearts pure and prevents resentment. Forgiveness toward ourselves absolves us of guilt and boosts our self-worth.

Forgiveness can affect our health and close the door to negative feelings. Beloved, the good news is that God, who instructed us to forgive, made the grace and power available to help us do so. In a nutshell, Jesus empowered us! Hallelujah! God will not command us to do what he has not empowered us for. Can we look at His provisions for us in helping us walk in forgiveness?

Walking in forgiveness by yielding to the Holy Spirit.

The Holy Spirit, who serves as our Advocate, Comforter, and Helper, is the Helper that Jesus promised to send before He went to heaven (John 14:16; 16:7 ESV). Whatever God has instructed us to do, including forgiving ourselves and others, is made possible and assisted by the Holy Spirit.

We must yield ourselves to the control of the Spirit to walk in forgiveness. We must spend time with God every morning before taking on the tasks of the day. As God starts to provide for our needs for the day, we pray, read the Bible, and pay attention to the voice of the Holy Spirit. Then, we can rely on Him to give us the strength and willingness to forgive when the time comes. Walking in forgiveness can be hard in the deficiency of our natural self because nobody wants to forgive someone who has hurt them. God, mercifully, has given us the ability for forgiveness.

Walking in Forgiveness by Obeying God's Word

"For the word of God is alive and active. Sharper than any double-edged sword, it penetrates even to dividing soul and spirit, joints and marrow; it judges the thoughts and attitudes of the heart." (Hebrews 4:12 NIV)

Saying you weren't mistreated or hurt in any manner is not the goal of forgiving someone or letting go. It's about walking in freedom, obeying God's Word, and deciding not to harbor a grudge against the offender. Reading aloud from Scripture personalized to you, reflecting on God's Word, and putting what you read and hear from the Holy Spirit will help you activate that grace, i.e., empowerment to forgive.

The same kindness and mercy that our Father bestows upon us should also be shown to the one who has harmed us. Jeremiah reminds us of God's kindness, compassion, and fidelity to us in Lamentations 3:22–23. "Through the Lord's mercies, we are not consumed, Because His compassions fail not. They are new every morning; Great is Your faithfulness." (Lamentations 3:22-23 NKJV). God's word opens us to the realities in Christ and our realities in Him. When we constantly behold God's word, we become what we read.

Walking in forgiveness by seeing the good in the offense

Our experiences and reactions to the obstacles in life are shaped by our perspectives. We regain the ability to turn suffering into purpose and resentment into compassion when we decide to find the positive aspects of the offense. Philippians 4:8 (NIV), which exhorts us to concentrate on things that are true, noble, right, pure, beautiful, and admirable, is in line with this point of view. Seeing the good in the offense doesn't mean trivializing or ignoring the harm caused. Instead, it involves shifting our perspective to recognize the potential lessons, growth opportunities, and blessings that can emerge from difficult situations.

Examples which include:

1. Personal Growth: Character development and personal growth are frequently sparked by adversity. We are taught in Romans 5:3-4 (NIV), "Not only so, but we also glory in our sufferings, because we know that suffering produces perseverance; perseverance, character; and character, hope." We can develop maturity and resilience by forgiving others.

2. Empathy and Compassion: Being harmed might increase our empathy and compassion for others who are in need. We are urged to "be kind and compassionate to one another, forgiving each other, just as in Christ God forgave you" (Ephesians 4:32 NIV).

3. Healing Relationships: Reconciliation and relationship repair can be enabled by forgiveness. According to Proverbs 17:9 (NIV), "Whoever would foster love covers over an offense, but whoever repeats the matter separates close friends." Deciding to find the positive aspects of the transgression might help people come to terms with it and develop a greater sense of mutual understanding.

This perspective makes it clear that the victim of the offense itself suffers more consequences from unforgiveness than benefits. Therefore, it is fantastic that we will essentially live above offense—not because of the offender, but because of ourselves. I have faith in Jesus Christ, that he will strengthen our hearts and prepare us for paradise even while we walk this path of holiness.

CHAPTER 6

MANAGING REJECTION

"Blessed are you when people hate you, when they exclude you and insult you and reject your name as evil, because of the Son of Man. Rejoice in that day and leap for joy, because great is your reward in heaven. For that is how their ancestors treated the prophets." - Luke 6:22-23 (NIV)

Rejection is a common experience, experienced by people of various races, ethnicities, countries, and continents. It is often accompanied by feelings of inadequacy, shame, and despair, leading us to question our decisions, worth, and purpose. There are two things you and I were never designed to experience: death and rejection. That is why they both feel so foreign and hurt so much; they are so contrary to what we were made for. When God created the world, everything in it was "very good" (Gen. 1:31). Neither physical death nor the death of relationships was part of his perfect design. But when mankind fell into sin, both experiences invaded our lives, tampering with our original identity (Gen. 3:16-24).

Adam and Eve rejected God and passed on a legacy of physical and relational death to their posterity. Cain rejected Abel as he slew him. Jacob rejected Leah and infected his household with jealousy. His sons rejected Joseph and broke their father's heart. And so, the narrative goes throughout Scripture ... including the dark night when Peter rejected Jesus as he walked alone to his death.

Most of us have had experiences that hurt far more than mine, experiences that define who we are now. A long-time friend turns his back on you. A stranger disparages your race or family. An employer demotes or fires you. A parent or child won't return your calls. Worst of all, a spouse says, "I don't want to live with you anymore." A married child vacations more often with her in-laws than with you. A pastor fails to visit when you're sick or struggling. A church member says your sermons aren't feeding him anymore. A boss dismisses a proposal or promotes someone else instead of you. A spouse prefers to work late, watch television, play video games, or focus on his smartphone rather than enjoy your company. Or someone criticizes your words, ideas, looks, or parenting. The closer the relationship, the greater the pain and the more rejection feels like death.

More so, even brethren in the bible were not left out of this phase of life. So, no matter how close we are to God, it will still hurt when other people reject us or things we value. David knew God intimately but was still devastated when a close friend betrayed him (Ps. 55:12-14). Paul saw Jesus face-to-face and consecrated his very life to him, and yet he was grieved over and over when churches he'd planted rejected his teaching (Gal. 4:19-20).

As people of faith, we are called to lean on our belief and trust in God's plan for our lives. "The Lord is close to the brokenhearted and saves those who are crushed in spirit" Psalm 34:18. Even in our darkest moments of rejection, God is present, offering comfort, strength, and hope. By surrendering our pain and disappointment to Him, we can find solace in the midst of rejection and emerge more robust and resilient.

The Identity Makers, Good Rejection vs. Bad Rejection

The story of Joseph in the Book of Genesis provides a powerful example of good rejection. Despite being sold into slavery by his own brothers and facing numerous trials and tribulations, Joseph remained faithful to God. Genesis 50:20 captures Joseph's perspective on his rejection: "You intended to harm me, but God intended it for good to accomplish what is now being done, the saving of many lives." On the other hand, bad rejection stems from a place of injustice, prejudice, or cruelty. When rejection is based on factors such as race, gender, or socioeconomic status, it not only inflicts pain but also perpetuates systems of oppression and inequality. As Christians, we are called to stand against such forms of rejection and advocate for justice and equality. Micah 6:8 exhorts us, "He has shown you, O mortal, what is good. And what does the Lord require of you? To act justly, love mercy, and walk humbly with your God."

Moreover, Jesus himself experienced rejection during his earthly ministry. He was despised and rejected by men, acquainted with grief and sorrow (Isaiah 53:3). Yet, through his rejection, Jesus brought salvation to the world. His sacrificial love demonstrates that God's redemptive power is at work despite the most profound rejection.

Let me quickly say here that rejection does not define you. Being rejected does not necessarily mean there is a problem with you, but maybe it just was not the right fit for the person making the decision, and that is also okay. This is the verse on my mind as I write this: 11 For I know the plans I have for you," declares the Lord, "plans to prosper you and not to harm you, plans to give you hope and a future. 12 Then you will call on me and come and pray to me, and I will listen to you. 13 You will seek me and find me when you seek me with all your heart. - Jeremiah 29:11.

I know rejection is painful, and I am not disputing it, but I also hope that this story might be the encouragement you need today to trust a good God with your future and the reminder that seasons will change. Your tears will turn into laughter in Jesus' Name. Amen!!

Dealing with this phase of life called Rejection

Scripture provides us with guidance and encouragement to deal with rejection. In Isaiah 41:10, we are reminded, "So do not fear, for I am with you; do not be dismayed, for I am your God. I will strengthen you and help you; I will uphold you with my righteous right hand." This is an assurance that even in our darkest moments, God is there to offer us His strength and support. Moreover, in Philippians 4:6-7, we are encouraged to bring our worries, rejections, and anxieties to God in prayer: "Do not be anxious about anything but in every situation, by prayer and petition, with thanksgiving, present your requests to God. And the peace of God, which transcends all understanding, will guard your hearts and your minds in Christ Jesus." You would see here that prayer is a powerful tool that can help us find peace and clarity in the midst of rejection. Let us trust God and His plan for our lives.

Moreover, in all these, what is the role of the gospel in transforming lives and reversing rejections? The gospel of Christ is the greatest example the world has ever seen of overcoming rejection. Colossians 1:19-22 declares: For in [Jesus] all the fullness of God was pleased to dwell, and through him to reconcile to himself all things, whether on earth or in heaven, making peace by the blood of his cross. And you, who once were alienated and hostile in mind, doing evil deeds, he has now reconciled in his body of flesh by his death to present you holy and blameless and above reproach before him; although mankind rejected God, God did not reject us. Even though we have sinned against God and gone our way, he is a faithful shepherd. He sent his Son Jesus into this world to seek what was lost, to offer himself up as a sacrifice for all our sins, and to open a path for reconciliation with our heavenly Father.

Through his Word, he has given us practical guidance on reversing rejection (see Rom. 15:5-7; Eph. 2:14-22; Eph. 4:30-32; Col. 3:12-15). Through his Spirit, God has given us the power to overcome our judgments, fears, and bitterness and to clothe ourselves with the patience, humility, gentleness, and courage of Christ as we do whatever we can to reverse the rejections we've caused or experienced until our identity in God is fulfilled. We cannot control how others will respond to our efforts, but out of love for Christ, we can do all we can to live at peace with others (Rom. 12:18). What they do in response is between them and God.

Even Now, God still loves and Accepts You

I wish I could say loudly to you that God's love is unchanging, far beyond our failures and shortcomings. In these truths, we find comfort amid rejection and embrace our true identity as beloved children of God. Scripture says in Romans 8:38-39, "For I am convinced that neither death nor life, neither angels nor demons, neither the present nor the future, nor any powers, neither height nor depth nor anything else in all creation, will be able to separate us from the love of God that is in Christ Jesus our Lord." This truth confirmed the unbreakable bond between God and His children, telling us that nothing, not even rejection, can separate you and me from His love.

Furthermore, Ephesians 2:4-5 again emphasizes, "But because of his great love for us, God, who is rich in mercy, made us alive with Christ even when we were dead in transgressions, it is by grace you have been saved." This verse reminds us that God's love is not based on our merit or worthiness but rather on His infinite mercy and grace. Even in our moments of rejection, God's love remains constant, offering us forgiveness, redemption, and a new life in Christ. As we internalize the truth of God's love for us, we are empowered to live boldly and authentically, free from the fear of rejection or condemnation. For God has not given us the spirit of fear but of power, love, and sound mind. Through the power of the Holy Spirit, we can overcome the challenge of rejection, heal, grow, and walk confidently in our true identity as beloved children of God.

For you who must deal with rejection, remember that God has perfected all that concerns you. One or many rejections do not define you when you know that God has promised that his plans for you are good. As you deal with your emotions, you can do a few things that may help you prepare for the right opportunity:

1) Learn and improve your skills: What can you learn that is relevant to the opportunity you want?

2) Ask other people for advice: ask and you shall be given; you and I need many people for advice at various points in our lives.

3) Remember that God is the Author and Finisher of your life, so continue to lean on him for direction and guidance. This is the time to go deeper in intimacy by studying the Word, praying, listening to messages, etc. You might find that God has an entirely different plan or purpose for your life, or you might find a new direction on how to approach a situation.

4) Gratitude: This is not just a thinking thing but a speaking thing. Speak thanks for when you wake up for what you do have and what you don't.

Managing rejection on a progressive scale involves understanding its effects and implementing strategies to counteract its negative impact. Rejection can manifest in various forms, such as loneliness, self-pity, misery, depression, despair, and even thoughts of death or suicide. Additionally, it can lead to emotional hardness, indifference, rebellion, and in extreme cases, involvement in witchcraft. However, the opposite of rejection is favor, which can be cultivated through various biblical principles and examples.

Understanding the Effects of Rejection

1. Loneliness: Rejection often leads to feelings of isolation and loneliness, as individuals may believe they are unworthy of connection or companionship.

 2. Self-pity: Those who experience rejection may indulge in self-pity, constantly dwelling on their perceived shortcomings or the unfairness of their circumstances.

3. Misery: Rejection can breed a sense of constant unhappiness and dissatisfaction with life, making it difficult to find joy or contentment.

4. Depression: Prolonged rejection can contribute to clinical depression, characterized by persistent feelings of sadness, hopelessness, and worthlessness.

5. Despair: Repeated rejection can lead to a sense of hopelessness about the future, making individuals feel as though they will never escape their current circumstances.

6. Death/Suicide: In severe cases, rejection may lead to thoughts of death or suicide as individuals struggle to cope with overwhelming feelings of pain and despair.

7. Hardness: Some individuals may develop emotional hardness as a defense mechanism against further rejection, making it challenging for them to form meaningful connections with others.

8. Indifference: Repeated rejection can also lead to a sense of indifference towards oneself and others, as individuals may numb themselves to avoid experiencing further pain.

9. Rebellion: Feelings of rejection may fuel rebellion against authority figures or societal norms, as individuals seek to assert their independence or regain a sense of control.

10. Witchcraft: In extreme cases, individuals may turn to witchcraft or other occult practices in a misguided attempt to gain power or control over their circumstances.

Strategies for Managing Rejection

1. Embrace Your Identity in Christ: Recognize that your worth and identity are found in Christ, not in the opinions or actions of others (Ephesians 1:6).

2. Follow Christ's Example: Look to the example of Christ, who grew in favor with both God and man (Luke 2:52), demonstrating humility, grace, and love even in the face of rejection.

3. Learn from Biblical Examples: Study the lives of biblical figures like Joseph, who experienced rejection and betrayal yet remained faithful to God, ultimately experiencing His favor (Genesis 39:4, 21).

4. Seek Wisdom: Pursue wisdom, which is the key to finding favor with both God and man (Proverbs 8:35). Seek God's guidance and direction in every aspect of your life.

5. Cultivate Mercy and Truth: Embrace the principles of mercy and truth, which lead to favor and good understanding in the sight of God and man (Proverbs 3:3-4).

6. Build Healthy Relationships with Authority: Develop respectful and supportive relationships with authority figures, recognizing the importance of honoring and submitting to God-ordained authority (Proverbs 16:15).

7. Seek a Life Partner: For those who desire marriage, seek a spouse by biblical principles, understanding that finding a good wife or husband is a sign of God's favor (Proverbs 18:22).

Remember that rejection is not the end of the story; it is an opportunity for growth, resilience, and ultimately, experiencing the abundant life that God desires for His children.

CHAPTER 7

DELIVERANCE

"For he has rescued us from the dominion of darkness and
brought us into the kingdom of the Son he loves"
(Colossians 1:13 NIV).

In a spiritual sense, "deliverance" means being freed from
servitude, oppression, or any other kind of captivity by the
power of God. It entails being free from spiritual
strongholds such as emotional loads, addictions,
generational curses, and demonic influences. To walk in
your true identity, you need to experience deliverance. The
first and most important deliverance is salvation. The Bible
says, "For he has rescued us from the dominion of darkness
and brought us into the kingdom of the Son he loves"
(Colossians 1:13 NIV).

Darkness is a state of confusion, and lack of clarity. It is the
absence of light. It is a place of depression and stagnancy.
Your false identity is like darkness, it keeps you away from

your authentic self. God rescued you from the dominion of darkness. It was a great deliverance. He brought you into the kingdom of His dear Son, the kingdom of light. It is difficult to identify people when they are in the darkness. You can't see yourself not talk of seeing others. It is a place of gloom. Now that you are in the light, God has brought you out of your past, shame, and confusion, so you can live out your true identity, and that is what true deliverance is all about. People who are bound in physical prisons across the world are little compared to the population of people roaming around free, but yet in the bondage of false identity.

Deliverance is the process of moving someone from a state of sin, negativity, or devastation into one of safety, strength, and spiritual healing. The Bible assures us that God hears our prayers and answers, restoring what is lost. Fighting spiritual battles and leading a victorious life include praying for rescue from adversity and evil.

The idea of deliverance is emphasized throughout the Bible, especially in the teachings of Jesus Christ. It is believed that Jesus is the ultimate deliverer, possessing the authority and capacity to release individuals from various ills. Jesus helped people in need by healing them, driving out devils, and restoring them during his time. The Bible assures Christians that God can set them free from spiritual slavery and provide them with direction, encouragement, and promises of escape.

God promises to set us free from all forms of slavery, including addiction, fear, unbelief and doubt, intense grief, resentment and unforgiveness, illness and disease, debt, demon possession and oppression, etc. God assured Moses in Exodus 3 that He would send him to deliver His people from Egypt. The Lord declared, "I have seen the misery of my people in Egypt," according to Exodus 3:7–10 ESV:

Then the Lord said, "I have surely seen the affliction of my people who are in Egypt and have heard their cry because of their taskmasters. I know their sufferings, and I have come down to deliver them out of the hand of the Egyptians and to bring them up out of that land to a good and broad land, a land flowing with milk and honey, to the place of the Canaanites, the Hittites, the Amorites, the Perizzites, the Hivites, and the Jebusites. And now, behold, the cry of the people of Israel has come to me, and I have also seen the oppression with which the Egyptians oppress them. Come, I will send you to Pharaoh that you may bring my people, the children of Israel, out of Egypt." Individuals frequently find themselves in challenging and hazardous situations. These postures can be spiritual or bodily at different times. It is necessary to deliver such a person.

In the Bible, deliverance can take many different forms. The Lord occasionally spares people from His wrath. These people would be Lot, who was spared from the judgment of Sodom and Gomorrah, and Noah, who was rescued from the Great Flood. God frequently freed the twelve tribes— the offspring of Abraham, Isaac, and Jacob—from difficult political and military circumstances once they had established themselves as a people. He rescued people from perilous circumstances.

A Canaanite lady, described in Matthew 15, came up to Jesus and his followers and begged him to save her severely suffering daughter, who was controlled by a demon. But Jesus didn't respond to her at first. Matthew 15:21–28 contains the story. At first, Jesus declined to assist her, stating that He had come to tend to Israel's lost sheep and that it was unfair to take the children's bread and give it to the tiny dogs or the Gentiles. Children's Bread symbolizes the blessings, provisions, and healing that God offers to His people, reflecting His love, compassion, and abundance.

Jesus was emphasizing that the Jews should receive the gospel first. The woman was prepared to accept crumbs because she understood what Jesus implied. She refused to accept no, and due to her strong faith, Jesus responded. One of the covenantal blessings associated with Jesus Christ is deliverance. Since we are Abraham's offspring and promised heirs, deliverance is also our share. According to John 1:12-13, "Yet to all who did receive him, to those who believed in his name, he gave the right to become children of God— children born not of natural descent, nor of human decision or a husband's will, but born of God."

Galatians 3:7-9 TPT says, "So the true children of Abraham have the same faith as their father! And the Scripture prophesied that by faith God would declare Gentiles to be righteous. God announced the good news ahead of time to Abraham: "Through your example of faith, all the nations will be blessed!" And so, the blessing of Abraham's faith is now our blessing, too! These scriptures unequivocally demonstrate that our sonship, which resulted from our faith in Jesus Christ, is what puts us into God's economy of blessings. Because of our salvation, we became sons of Abraham and inherited a share of Christ's inheritance, in which deliverance is one and major of it.

Therefore, it is necessary to be totally free from all that ties us to the world so we can fully experience the blessing of becoming one with Christ. Jesus' assignment to his followers to go out into the world and share the gospel with people first makes sense. Everything else was secondary to Jesus' primary goal of saving the unbelievers. Deliverance, blessings, healing, and other such occurrences would be an afterthought or reaction to the first gift of salvation.

Deliverance was referred to by Jesus as "children's bread." This is for believers, not for unbelievers! The good news is that you are eligible for deliverance if you have been saved. Children's Bread emphasizes that God's benefits are available to everyone who approaches Him in faith, reflecting the inclusion of God's mercy and supply. These ideas uphold the status of believers as God's children, heirs to His promises, and beneficiaries of His boundless kindness and love.

The idea of Deliverance being Children's Bread captures a major essence of the Christian message, which is that God is a kind and gracious Father who extends an invitation to His children to find abundant life, healing, and freedom via trust in Jesus Christ. Adopting these principles gives believers the ability to live victorious lives, extending

God's love and grace to others and taking part in the continuous process of world reconciliation and redemption.

Deliverance is for Christians, not for unbelievers. Its purpose is to set free believers who might be held captive by demonic forces, not to solve all the world's problems.

Jesus referenced the prophet Isaiah 61:1-3 in Luke 4:18–19 KJV The Spirit of the Lord is upon me, Because he hath anointed me to preach the gospel to the poor; He hath sent me to heal the brokenhearted, to preach deliverance to the captives, And recovering of sight to the blind, To set at liberty them that are bruised, To preach the acceptable year of the Lord. Jesus came with the mission to rescue us, God's children, from all forms of injustice, slavery, and danger.

Matthew 15:26 However, in response, he stated, "It is improper to take the children's bread and throw it to the dogs." Could He have been implying that it is improper to provide deliverance to those who do not believe? He called anyone who was not part of the covenant, which at the time included Gentiles, "dogs." The covenant does not apply to the unsaved of today. To be a part of the covenant, you have to believe in Jesus!

We witness how God saves his people - the Israelites, who are the same people as the Christians of the New Testament, right from the beginning of the Old Testament. Numerous stories found in both the Old and New Testaments illustrate how God provides for his people—even entire nations. A powerful testimony of God's faithfulness in delivering His people can be found in the stories of Shadrach, Meshach, and Abednego, the three Hebrew men, and Daniel in the lion's den. These events show the idea of the "children's bread" that Jesus promised and act as ageless reminders of heavenly care and provision.

God moved quickly and miraculously to help. The lions were fierce and hungry, but they did not hurt Daniel. His deliverance resulted from his loyalty and trust in the Almighty. The den turned what appeared to be certain death into an exhibit of miraculous deliverance, serving as a monument to God's might and protection. The story of Shadrach, Meshach, and Abednego serves as an example of enduring faith in the face of hardship in a similar manner. They faced the fury of King Nebuchadnezzar when they refused to submit to the golden image, and he gave them the command to be thrown into the blazing furnace.

The words "Our God whom we serve is able to deliver us from the burning fiery furnace, and He will deliver us from your hand, O king" resounds through the passage of time with bravery and trust (Daniel 3:17). The core of the children's bread is embodied in their persistent confidence in God's deliverance, even at the cost of confronting death—divine provision and protection for His faithful ones. God is more than willing to provide us with deliverance beyond our wildest expectations. It comes as part of his package when we accept salvation. It is not expected of any Child of God to be limited. It must not be disregarded!

Embrace Freedom and Wholeness

Sometimes, we often find ourselves burdened by the weight of our past, entangled in toxic relationships, and ensnared by negative situations that hinder our growth and limit our potential. Yet, amidst the struggles and challenges we face, there is a promise of healing and deliverance; a promise that offers hope and restoration to those who dare to believe.

As explained earlier, the notion that healing and deliverance are the children's bread finds its origin in the teachings of Jesus Christ. In the Gospel of Matthew, we find Jesus proclaiming these words to a Canaanite woman who came to Him seeking healing for her demon-possessed daughter. Despite being initially rebuffed by Jesus, the woman persisted in her faith, declaring, "Yes, Lord, yet even the dogs eat the crumbs that fall from their masters' table" (Matthew 15:27, ESV). Moved by her unwavering faith, Jesus granted her request, affirming the truth that healing and deliverance are not exclusive privileges reserved for a select few but are accessible to all who come to Him in faith.

This encounter serves as a powerful reminder of God's unfailing love and compassion towards His children. It highlights the inclusive nature of His grace, which knows no bounds and extends to all who call upon His name. Just as a loving parent provides nourishment and sustenance for their children, so too does our Heavenly Father offer healing and deliverance as the bread of life, satisfying the deepest longings of our souls and bringing restoration to every area of our lives.

Breaking Free from the Grip of the Past

One of the most significant obstacles to experiencing healing and deliverance is the grip of the past. Past wounds, traumas, and regrets often haunt us, casting a shadow over our present and robbing us of joy and peace. Whether it be the pain of past relationships, the scars of past mistakes, or the trauma of past experiences, the past has a way of holding us captive, preventing us from moving forward and embracing the abundant life that God has promised.

Yet, the good news is that through Christ, we have been given the power to break free from the chains of the past. The Apostle Paul writes in 2 Corinthians 5:17, "Therefore, if anyone is in Christ, he is a new creation. The old has passed away; behold, the new has come" (ESV). In Christ, we are no longer defined by our past failures or shortcomings but are given a new identity as sons and daughters of God, redeemed and restored by His grace.

To experience healing and deliverance from the grip of the past, you must first acknowledge the pain and brokenness that you carry. You must bring your hurts and burdens to the foot of the cross, surrendering them to Jesus and allowing His healing touch to bring restoration to your wounded heart. This process may require vulnerability and transparency, as you open yourself up to God's transformative work in your life.

Additionally, you must choose to forgive those who have wronged you, as previously shared, releasing the bitterness and resentment that have taken root in your heart. Forgiveness is not condoning the actions of others but rather choosing to extend grace and mercy as you have received from God. As you forgive others, you open the door for God's healing power to flow freely in your life, breaking the chains of unforgiveness and setting you free from the bondage of the past.

Embracing Freedom from Toxic Relationships

In addition to the grip of the past, toxic relationships can also hinder your experience of healing and deliverance. Whether it be friendships, family dynamics, or romantic entanglements, toxic relationships have a way of draining us emotionally, mentally, and spiritually, leaving us feeling depleted and disillusioned. These relationships often perpetuate cycles of dysfunction and codependency, keeping us trapped in patterns of behavior that are harmful to our well-being.

However, God desires for us to experience freedom and wholeness in our relationships. He desires for us to surround ourselves with people who uplift and encourage us, rather than tear us down and hold us back. The Apostle Paul writes in 2 Corinthians 6:14, "Do not be unequally yoked with unbelievers. For what partnership has righteousness with lawlessness? Or what fellowship has light with darkness?" (ESV). This admonition reminds us of the importance of choosing relationships that align with God's purposes and values, relationships that bring life and not death.

To experience healing and deliverance from toxic relationships, we must first discern which relationships are life-giving and which are draining. This requires honest introspection and a willingness to confront difficult truths about the dynamics of our relationships. It may also require setting healthy boundaries and creating distance from those who consistently bring negativity and toxicity into our lives.

Additionally, we must cultivate healthy relationship habits, such as effective communication, active listening, and mutual respect. When we prioritize open and honest communication, we create space for healing and reconciliation in our relationships, fostering a spirit of unity and understanding. We must also seek God's guidance and wisdom in navigating difficult relationships, trusting Him to lead us into paths of righteousness and peace.

Discovering Purpose and Wholeness in God's Plan

Ultimately, the journey of healing and deliverance leads us into a future of wholeness and purpose - a future shaped by God's divine plan for our lives. Jeremiah 29:11 declares, "For I know the plans I have for you, declares the Lord, plans for welfare and not for evil, to give you a future and a hope" (ESV). This promise reminds us that God has a purpose and a destiny for each one of us, a plan that far exceeds our wildest dreams and expectations.

To discover your purpose and wholeness in God's plan, you must first surrender your life fully to Him, trusting in His sovereignty and goodness. You must allow Him to heal your brokenness and restore your soul, empowering you to walk in freedom and confidence. This may require stepping out in faith and obedience, as you follow God's leading and direction for your life.

Additionally, you must seek to align your desires and ambitions with God's purposes, seeking His will above all else. This may involve letting go of your plans and agendas, surrendering them to God's higher purposes, and trusting in His perfect timing. As you yield yourself to God's will, you position yourself to receive His blessings and favor, walking in the fullness of His plan for your life.

CHAPTER 8

WALKING IN FAITH

"For we walk by faith, not by sight." - 2 Corinthians 5:7

Among several experiences of my life's journey, I realized I needed to embrace 'faith' as a part of my identity in Christ. From the deep pains of life and the depths of my soul, I recall the words that console me from Hebrews 11:1, "Now faith is confidence in what we hope for and assurance about what we do not see." These words are the echoes, the lyrics, and the sounds in the corridors of my heart; they resonate with the truth that faith is not merely a fleeting sentiment, but a steadfast conviction rooted in the eternal promises of God.

Consider "faith" as the energy source that ignites our inner abilities and strengths, like the fuel to a vehicle; it is a guiding belief system, enabling us to unlock our latent potential and achieve remarkable feats. Within this belief framework, individuals are called upon to trust a divine being or higher power, even though they cannot be perceived with our physical senses. Indeed, it's often more straightforward to have confidence in tangible, visible entities, particularly for those who place great value on their intellect and reasoning abilities. Nevertheless, faith transcends mere abstract concepts; it serves as a cornerstone in the Bible, speaking throughout its pages a remarkable 458 times in the New International translation. This frequent mention underscores its pivotal role and highlights its profound importance in guiding believers' lives.

One essential component of the Christian life is walking in faith. It entails living by God's Word, obeying His instructions, and putting your faith in His promises. What, then, is Faith? The Bible says, "NOW FAITH is the assurance (the confirmation, the title deed) of the things [we] hope for, being the proof of things, [we] do not see and the conviction of their reality [faith perceiving as real fact what is not revealed to the senses]" (Hebrews 11:1 AMPC). The Passion Translation says, "Now faith brings our hopes into reality and becomes the foundation needed to acquire the things we long for. It is all the evidence required to prove what is still unseen."

From these various Bible versions, there is one thing that remains unchanged. It is the fact that faith is trust! Seeing the possibilities in impossibilities. Being able to capture an essence that seems unrealistic into reality. Faith, some say, is a risk, but I see faith as seeing through the lens of God himself. The Greek term pistis is translated as "faith" in the New Testament into English. Pistis is used of belief with the predominant idea of trust (or confidence), whether in God or Christ, springing from faith in the same," according to the New Strong's Expanded Dictionary of Bible Words. "Faith" refers to assurance, belief, trust, and confidence (p. 1315).

The assurance or substance of things we hope for but have not yet received is faith. Our evidence of the unseen, the spiritual and invisible things, also comes from faith (confidence, belief, trust). Before a person's desire is granted by God or before their prayer is heard, faith is necessary. Faith is not necessary if we have gotten what we prayed for. To walk in faith is to submit to God's will continually, have faith in His promises, and depend on Him for support and direction in all facets of our lives. We encounter the accomplishment of God's plans and an unfathomable serenity as we develop and fortify our faith via prayer, the Bible, and obedience.

Faith, friends, goes beyond merely professing the Bible. Many Christians think that by having faith, they can force God to do something that he does not want to. Faith is listening to God speak to you about a problem and clinging to His word(s) when it appears hopeless. It is more than merely choosing a verse from the Bible that fits your circumstances. In its most authentic form, faith is a very personal journey characterized by close interactions with God's live Word, going beyond the simple recital of beliefs. As Christians, we are called to live according to the truth of God, which is revealed to us personally, resonates with our spirit, and is publicly expressed through our faith. There is always a question that faith poses to u, "What has God said to you concerning this situation"? What have you heard from God? A verse of the scripture states this (Romans 10:17 TPT).

Faith, then, is birthed in a heart that responds to God's anointed utterance of the Anointed One. Faith is a response to the declarations and statements of God. God's word remains the foundation or the basis upon which Faith is built and established. The nature of faith is succinctly expressed by the author in Hebrews 11:1, "Now faith is confidence in what we hope for and assurance about what we do not see." Here, faith is shown as an active confidence that is based on the unseen truths of God's promises rather than as a passive acknowledgment. It is a belief that is grounded on God's immutable nature and transcends empirical proof.

We read about people in Scripture whose lives were changed by direct contact with God's word. When Moses encountered the burning bush in the Old Testament, God spoke to him immediately and asked him to lead the Israelites out of slavery (Exodus 3:1–12). Moses' faith was sparked by a personal insight rather than just a supernatural mandate, which initiated the nation's redemption. In a similar vein, the lives of the disciples in the New Testament demonstrate the transforming power of intimate interaction. Jesus asks his disciples a crucial question in Matthew 16:15–16: "But what about you?" Who do you think I am?" In addition to expressing his belief, Peter's reply, "You are the Messiah, the Son of the living God," is a deep revelation from the Father (Matthew 16:17).

In addition, Saul's encounter with God on the way to Damascus serves as an example of the profound change that happens when God's truth and human experience collide (Acts 9:1-19). The rising Christ gave Saul, a persecutor of the early church, a startling insight that completely changed the course of his life. An ardent gospel apostle was born, not from a simple intellectual conversion but from a heavenly encounter.

Faith for Living

Faith is not merely a belief or a feeling; it is a way of life, a journey of trust and obedience, a path of surrender and sacrifice. While belief isn't the same as faith, it's the starting point. Belief is the sense that something is true. But like trust, firm belief must be combined with trust and action to hold real value. What good is believing it will rain if you don't bring an umbrella? Similarly, within the Christian faith, what good is believing in God if you don't love Him, live by faith, and follow His commandments? So, if I claim to believe, it means that Jesus' life, teachings, and character shape my actions. It guides how I treat others, respect communities, and engage with nations. That's why I serve in Jesus' name and dedicate myself to helping needy children because of my faith. Some individuals view faith simply as a religious association or a sense of reassurance from a higher power for their loyalty. However, the scriptures in the Bible depict it as something deeper: a profound trust in God, even in His unseen presence. When I first encountered this concept, I found myself drawn to it. Living in a manner that transcended the limits of what I could physically perceive presented a challenge. The Bible instructs us to lead our lives guided by faith rather than solely relying on what is visible and tangible, which goes against conventional thinking. So, how do I distinguish myself as someone who adheres to these principles in a world that predominantly operates based on what is observable and concrete? As a result, this way of life, I refer to as faith, is acquired through understanding gained from hearing teachings or explanations rooted in the teachings of Jesus Christ found in the Holy Scriptures, the divine wisdom.

Walking in faith is a lifelong process that transforms our lives until we eventually meet Jesus. It is not a one-time occurrence. It is a journey characterized by faith, tenacity, and steadfast confidence in God's promises. 2 Corinthians 5:7 urges us to walk by faith, not by sight. Our journey in faith requires us to trust in God's guidance even when we cannot see the path ahead clearly. Like Peter stepping out of the boat to walk on water, our faith requires us to take bold steps, trusting that God will sustain us even amid life's storms (Matthew 14:29).

Hebrews 10:36 exhorts us to hold fast to our faith since it is only by patient perseverance that we will be granted God's promises. We must hold fast to our beliefs in the face of difficulties and setbacks. The tale of Job serves as an example of how faith can endure unfathomable adversity. Ultimately, Job's unshakable faith in God brought about blessing and restoration (Job 42:10). Walking in faith is a constant act of trust and obedience as we go through life. Although the road is full of obstacles, disappointments, and victories, in the end, it brings us face-to-face with Jesus. Because our faith has become sight, let us focus on Him and hold fast to our faith until the day we see Him in person (1 Corinthians 13:12).

Living this way has influenced and continues to impact my words, actions, attitudes, public speaking, and demonstrations of spiritual power. It's important to note that faith isn't something you receive as a gift that can be given too; it's a deliberate characteristic that believers must embody as they navigate life. It's about relying on something intangible, 'trust'. This trust is placed in the divine being, the immortal, through a conscious decision, a risk, even though you haven't seen Him with your physical eyes throughout your life. Furthermore, those who witness this lifestyle and live out this example are Christians who go beyond mere trust. Their faith extends beyond trust; trusting in the Word of God is an active expression of faith. As we tread the paths of life, I would also have you know that walking in faith is not merely a destination to be reached but a journey to be embraced. It is a journey marked by trust, perseverance, and unwavering hope, guided by the eternal promise of God's faithfulness. With each step, just like I told myself, you must also embrace this sacred call to walk in faith, knowing that He who began a good work in you will carry it on to completion until the day of Christ Jesus (Philippians 1:6).

The road of faith is not smooth or without its share of trials and tribulations. There will be moments of doubt and uncertainty, moments when the storms of life threaten to overwhelm me. But in those moments, I will cling to the unwavering promise of God's faithfulness, knowing that He who has called me is faithful, and He will surely do it (1 Thessalonians 5:24). I will trust in His unfailing love, knowing that nothing can separate me from His love (Romans 8:38-39). So, I will walk boldly, with my eyes fixed on Jesus, the author and perfecter of my faith (Hebrews 12:2). I will trust in His unfailing love, knowing that He will never leave me nor forsake me (Deuteronomy 31:6). And I will press on toward the goal to win the prize for which God has called me heavenward in Christ Jesus (Philippians 3:14). For He is my rock and my fortress, my deliverer and my shield; in Him, I take refuge (Psalm 18:2). And as I walk in faith, I know that He will guide me with His eye upon me (Psalm 32:8). So, I will wait on the Lord and be of good courage, for He shall strengthen my heart (Psalm 27:14). And in the end, I will stand before Him, clothed in the righteousness of Christ, and hear the words, "Well done, good and faithful servant; enter into the joy of your Lord" (Matthew 25:21).

The Walk of Faith

Everyone encounters moments where their trust must be put into action. Take, for instance, the story of Abraham binding Isaac. God tests Abraham's faith in this biblical account by instructing him to sacrifice his son, Isaac. God wanted to see Abraham's obedience in action. Despite his love for his son, Abraham had unwavering confidence, trust, belief, and faith in God, His goodness, and His divine plan for his family. God, who is faithful and merciful, sent an angel to spare Isaac's life just moments before Abraham was about to sacrifice him. As a reward for Abraham's obedience and faith, God promised to make his descendants as numerous as the stars in the sky. This promise stands for all who trust and walk in faith with God, knowing His blessings are available to those who trust His word. Therefore, we must trust Elohim, entirely relying on God.

By following Abraham's example of complete trust in God, we can better align our actions with God's commandments. In essence, having faith involves two aspects: trust and action. This is the wholeness of faithfulness. Being faithful means translating trust into action. This active faith is emphasized throughout the letter of James, where he stresses the link between faith and deeds. Good works don't save a sinner, but they do validate faith. When we accept Jesus Christ as our Savior, we invite Him to transform our spirit and behavior. Following this transformation, true faith is expected to manifest through the fruit of the Holy Spirit. We're called to demonstrate our faith through His grace and mercy. God expects us to defend the fatherless and not ignore the suffering of children. We must respond with faith in action.

In various situations, faithfulness can resemble loyalty. When you're faithful to someone, you show unwavering commitment to that person. However, if this loyalty is betrayed, it's termed as "breaking faith." Moreover, faithfulness can be demonstrated through diligence. For example, a dedicated employee who consistently fulfills their duties may be seen as faithful. Regardless of the context, being faithful is understood as an active quality.

Let me emphasize once more: faith is about the here and now. Biblically, it's defined as a steadfast trust in God. Those who have faith trust in the present because the God of heaven has proven Himself reliable with undeniable evidence throughout the Bible. Although not tangible, walking in faith is genuine, intentional, and conscious. This life of faith is sensible. While some may prefer superstitions, walking with God is a rational life grounded in reliable evidence. Paul found evidence for Jesus' resurrection that fell short of modern logic's demands, yet the supernatural truths of faith, while surpassing reason, do not contradict it. Truth cannot oppose truth, and the same God who gave us the gift of reason also inspires our principles, reflecting His divine truth.

This divine truth is how we win or survive this mortal realm; we live on the fact as a meal from the table of the divine one in the Trinity. I recall moments when life threw very challenging issues of doubt and fear when the shadows of adversity threatened to engulf me in despair. Yet, in those moments, I found solace in the words of truths in Psalm 23:4, "Even though I walk through the darkest valley, I will fear no evil, for you are with me; your rod and your staff, they comfort me." Amidst my trials, I clung to the promise of God's presence, knowing He would never leave or forsake me. As I reflect upon this journey of faith, I remember the countless examples of courage and resilience found within the pages of Scripture. From the steadfast faith of Abraham to the unwavering trust of David, who faced the giant Goliath with nothing but a sling and a stone, these stories serve as timeless reminders of the transformative power of walking in faith. Yet, this walking in faith is not confined to the pages of ancient history; it is alive and active.

I recall the story of a dear friend who battled cancer with unwavering faith, trusting in God's healing touch even in the face of uncertainty and metastasis progression. Though the journey was fraught with pain and struggle, her faith remained unshakeable, a beacon of hope amidst the darkness. She held on to the altar's four horns until God came through for her and received her healing by faith.

I think of Sarah, a young woman raised in a broken home who carried the weight of her past like a heavy burden, unsure of where she belonged or who she was meant to be. But amidst the darkness, a candle of hope ignited within her soul, a whisper of faith that beckoned her to trust in something greater than herself. As Sarah began to walk in faith, she soon discovered a newfound sense of purpose and belonging. With each step, she felt the weight of her past lifting, replaced by the lightness of God's grace and love. She found solace in the words of Jeremiah 29:11, "For I know the plans I have for you, declares the Lord, plans to prosper you and not to harm you, plans to give you hope and a future." These words became her anchor, building her faith and grounding her in the assurance that God had a great purpose for her life. Sarah's story, among others, is a testament to the transformative power of walking in faith. You can see God's extraordinary hand, shaping lives, transforming hearts, and redeeming brokenness. But walking in faith isn't always easy. It requires us to step out of our comfort zones and trust in God's timing and plan, even when it doesn't align with our own. It's a journey of uncertainty, doubt, hope, and promise.

So let us walk in faith, my friends, knowing we are not alone on this journey. For God is with us, guiding our steps, strengthening our hearts, and leading us into a future filled with hope and promise. And as we walk in faith, may we be a beacon of light to all those around us, shining brightly with the love and grace of our Heavenly Father.

CHAPTER 9

WALKING IN LOVE

Love your neighbor as yourself.' There is no commandment greater than these."

(Mark 12:30-31 NIV).

Walking in love is at the center of Christianity. This is not just about actions but also about the attitudes and choices that reflect God's love and compassionate regard for others. Throughout the Bible, love is emphasized repeatedly, showing its significance in the lives of believers and Christian communities. As you walk in your true identity, you need to walk in love. As a being, you are made to know, understand, communicate, and give love. So, understanding God's love is important in comprehending our identity, worth, and purpose. His love profoundly transforms us, giving us a sense of value that surpasses the world or social media can offer. When we recognize ourselves as children of God, we find our true significance.

Love is not just defined by the feeling of loving or being loved but also as a commandment of God. The Bible says, "Love the Lord your God with all your heart and with all your soul and with all your mind and with all your strength.' The second is this: 'Love your neighbor as yourself.' There is no commandment greater than these." (Mark 12:30-31 NIV).

God's love is the ultimate example; it serves as a guide for believers. When we emulate God's character, promises, and Word, we must deepen our relationship with Him, empowering us to live out our purpose freely. Drawing from God's boundless love, the Bible offers guidance on embodying love in our lives. According to Scripture, love lies at the core of God's nature. The Bible says, "Whoever does not love does not know God, because God is love." (1 John 4:8 NIV).

God's love is steadfast, sacrificial, and constant, far more than a fleeting emotion. Perhaps the most poignant expression of God's love is found in John 3:16: "For God so loved the world that he gave his one and only Son, that whoever believes in him shall not perish but have eternal life." It's crucial that we truly understand the essence of Love and what it truly entails. In one of his letters, the

Apostle Paul provides us with a clear picture of what Love embodies. In 1 Corinthians 13:4-8, Paul delineates the characteristics of love:

• Love is patient and kind.

• It does not envy, boast, or parade itself.

• It does not act haughtily or rudely.

• It is not self-centered, easily provoked, or resentful.

• It does not rejoice in wrongdoing but in truth.

• It bears all things, believes all things, hopes all things, endures all things.

• Love never fails; it does not diminish or fade away.

This passage teaches us that love is not merely a feeling, but a conscious choice demonstrated through actions and attitudes. This love is patient and kind, not driven by envy or pride. The same kind of love seeks the good of others, forgives readily, and perseveres through challenges. This model of love stands firm in truth and righteousness, never faltering or diminishing. God's given way of love life, as described here, is enduring and unwavering, a guiding light in our relationships and interactions.

God's love knows no boundaries; it transcends race, nationality, and background. It's not selective; it encompasses everyone, even those we may consider adversaries (Matthew 5:43-48). As believers, we must identify with God and reflect His boundless love in our relationships. This love isn't earned but freely given; we are its recipients. To walk in love, you should start from your convictions and willingness to live as Christ did. It's not about mimicking His gestures but embodying His beliefs and values. Walking in love entails surrendering to Christ entirely and desiring a closer relationship with Him and others. It's a journey of continuous growth, never settling for mere surface expressions of love.

We're urged not to grow complacent but to continually follow God's example of love. Ephesians 5:1-2 encourages us to imitate God as beloved children and walk in love, just as Christ loved us and sacrificed Himself for us. This admonition from Paul the Apostle underscores the importance of emulating God's love in our lives.

Jesus, our perfect example, demonstrated God's love by offering Himself as a sacrifice for humanity. His selfless act mirrors God's love for us despite our flaws and struggles. Following Jesus' example, we reflect God's love for others and honor our identity as His children. Just as Jesus lovingly gave Himself for us, we're called to love sacrificially and selflessly mirroring Jesus's love. In essence, walking in love defines our identity as children of God. When we imitate Jesus' sacrificial love, we honor God and embody His love in our interactions with others. It's not merely a declaration but a lifestyle, an ongoing journey of reflecting God's love to the world.

The essence of love is demonstrated through genuine care and concern for others' well-being. This transformation springs from a profound change in the heart and mind accompanying walking in love. Achieving this requires selflessness, humility, and forgiveness, traits Christ Himself exemplifies (Philippians 2:5-8). As followers of Christ, we're called to mirror His love in every aspect of our lives. Throughout the New Testament, Jesus emphasizes the importance of love as a foundational commandment for His disciples. In Matthew 22:37–39, He instructs us to love God with all our being and to love our neighbors as ourselves. These two principles encapsulate the essence of the Old Testament law and are non-negotiable in the Christian life.

Living out this love involves more than just sentimentality or verbal affirmations; it requires tangible acts of compassion, justice, and grace toward others. Jesus teaches us to be compassionate to the marginalized, to stand up for justice and morality, and to extend grace to those in need (Micah 6:8). In essence, walking in love means embodying Christ's mercy and compassion in our interactions with others. James 2:15-16 reminds us that true love is demonstrated through practical actions, not just empty words. Merely offering verbal well-wishes to those in need without providing tangible help falls short of genuine love. As believers, we're called to be active agents of love, meeting the practical needs of others and reflecting the compassion of Christ in our deeds.

Although crucial, walking in love isn't always easy. Various obstacles, like pride, selfishness, and unresolved conflicts, can hinder our ability to love unconditionally. These barriers can strain genuine relationships and stifle the expression of love. Thankfully, through God's transformative love, believers can overcome these challenges and extend grace and forgiveness to one another.

In Ephesians 4:32, Christians are commanded to be kind, tenderhearted, and forgiving toward one another, just as God forgave them through Christ. This directive underscores the responsibility believers have in restoring relationships and promoting reconciliation. When we embody God's grace and forgiveness, believers can mend broken bonds and foster unity within the Christian community.

More so, there are many examples of different individuals who have walked in love, demonstrating the very identity of every child of God. Some, even in the bible, learned love through pain or shame, but the same came to others quickly through grace. I remember Sarah, a woman whose heart overflowed with love for those in need. Despite facing her challenges, she dedicated her life to serving the homeless in her community. Every morning, rain or shine, she would rise before dawn to prepare hot meals and distribute warm blankets to those sleeping on the streets. Her acts of kindness were not just gestures; they were expressions of love that touched the hearts of many, offering hope in despair.

Then there's Michael, a man who learned the true meaning of love through forgiveness. Growing up, he harbored resentment towards his absent father, blaming him for the pain and hardships he endured. But as he matured in his faith, Michael realized that holding onto bitterness only imprisoned his heart. Through prayer and reflection, he found the strength to forgive his father, releasing the weight of anger and embracing the freedom that comes from extending grace. In that moment of forgiveness, Michael experienced the transformative power of love, healing wounds that had long been buried deep within his soul.

And who could forget Emily, a young woman whose life was forever changed by a simple act of kindness? After losing her job and struggling to make ends meet, she felt like she had hit rock bottom. But one day, a stranger approached her with a warm smile and a listening ear. They offered words of encouragement and a helping hand, restoring Emily's faith in humanity and reminding her that she was not alone. That encounter planted a seed of hope in Emily's heart, igniting a newfound passion to pay it forward and spread love to others in need.

These stories are just a glimpse of the countless lives touched and transformed by the power of walking in love. It's a journey that transcends boundaries and breaks down barriers, uniting hearts in a common bond of compassion and empathy. In a world often characterized by division and strife, walking in love is a revolutionary act of defiance. It's choosing to see the humanity in others, even when they may seem unlovable. It's extending grace and forgiveness, even in the face of betrayal and hurt. It's embracing the broken and the marginalized, offering a beacon of hope in a world shrouded in darkness. But perhaps most importantly, walking in love reflects the unconditional love that God has lavished upon us. It's recognizing that we are all beloved children of the Most High, created in His image and called to love one another as He has loved us.

As I reflect on these stories and the countless others like them, I am reminded of the words of 1 Corinthians 13:13, "And now these three remain: faith, hope, and love. But the greatest of these is love." In the end, it is love that binds us together, love that sustains us in times of trial, and love that ultimately prevails overall. So let us walk in love, dear friends, with hearts open wide and arms outstretched. In so doing, we embody the very essence of our identity in Christ, and we bear witness to the transformative power of love that has the potential to change the world.

CHAPTER 10

KNOWING GOD

"That I may know him, and the power of his resurrection, and the fellowship of his sufferings, being made conformable unto his death" (Philippians 3:10 KJV).

Have you ever wondered why Apostle Paul who was considered the "greatest" continued to express his desire to know Jesus even as he neared the end of his life on earth? It's a good question to ask: Is there a limit to how much we can learn about God, or can we become experts or "professors" of divine knowledge?

The Bible says, "That I may know him, and the power of his resurrection, and the fellowship of his sufferings, being made conformable unto his death" (Philippians 3:10 KJV). In this scriptural verse, Paul expresses his deep desire to know Christ intimately, experience the power of His resurrection, share in His sufferings, and become like Him in His death. It reflects Paul's yearning for a profound relationship with Jesus, not just knowing about Him intellectually but knowing Him intimately, experientially, and spiritually. Thirty years before, on the road to Damascus, Paul had experienced a tremendous encounter with Christ. Although he had several other encounters with Him since then, Paul yearned for a deeper relationship with Him. His example teaches us that there is always more to know the Lord, regardless of how long or how well we have known Him.

Paul's aspiration also underscores the depth of fellowship and communion he seeks with Christ, transforming his life and shaping his identity as a follower of Jesus. Paul's desire to know Christ paves the road for us in our current quest for knowledge of God. Through His Son, Jesus Christ, we see God most clearly and get to know Him most intimately. John 14:9 quotes Jesus as saying, "Whoever has seen me has seen the Father." Similarly, Col. 1:15, 19 says, "He is the image of the invisible God."

It's critical to realize that when we talk about knowing God, we're not talking about mystical experiences or abstract or theoretical ideas about God; instead, we're talking about coming alive to God via the instrumentality of the knowledge given through Jesus, his son. We must realize that knowing God is essential to living a Christian life - it is not optional. According to Jesus (John 17:3), this is eternal life "because they know you, the only true God, and Jesus Christ whom you have sent." The word "know" here refers to experiential knowledge rather than merely an intellectual comprehension of facts about God, Jesus, or the Bible.

It takes time to get to find out God more fully. It does not happen instantly. Paul had been aware of Christ for a long time when he stated that getting to know Christ better, as was already mentioned. He continued, saying, "Not as though I had already attained, either were already perfect: but I follow after if that I may apprehend that for which also I am apprehended of Christ Jesus. (Phil. 3:12) KJV. Furthermore, getting to know Christ better requires genuine work; it is not an effortless procedure. Is grace incompatible with effort? No. Grace does not mind labor; she is against earning (the law). A key component of how grace functions in sanctification is effort. Paul, the grace-apostle, continued by saying to the Philippians.

A tightly connected inner examination of God's qualities and deeds is necessary to truly know him; this leads to a passionate celebration of God's person and deeds and a fellowship with him. To know God is to diligently investigate the many ways that God has shown himself in Scripture. This relationship starts as soon as we become alive to God; that is when we are saved from the condition of eternal damnation into which all people are born and allowed to live forever if they put their faith in Jesus. Repentance is the first step in forgiving ourselves of our sins; faith is the second, which is placing our faith in Jesus and His sacrifice on his death cross to forgive us of our sins. You need both to come alive to God. Jesus said this was either born of the Holy Spirit or above. It denotes adoption into God's family and arrival in His realm (John 3:3–8). Some humans cannot see, comprehend, or understand God or His kingdom unless they are reborn by the Holy Spirit.

As said earlier, knowing God is not something mystical or hidden for or from a particular group of people. As much as we want to know God, God wants to make himself known to us. He desires that men know him. He is willing to open himself to us. Let's look into some of the ways God makes himself known.

1. Through Creation. The natural world's elegance, intricacy, and order frequently represent God's nature and qualities. In the pursuit of understanding the divine, nature stands as a profound testament to the existence and

attributes of God. As we delve into the intricacies of the natural world, we unravel layers of wisdom and beauty, each unveiling a glimpse of the divine essence.

In Psalm 19:1-4, the Bible proclaims, "The heavens declare the glory of God; the skies proclaim the work of his hands. Day after day they pour forth speech; night after night they reveal knowledge. They have no speech; they use no words; no sound is heard from them. Yet their voice goes out into all the earth, their words to the ends of the world." According to Romans 1:20, creation amply demonstrates God's omnipotence and divine essence; hence, humanity has no justification for denying Him.

2. Through Scripture: The Bible is the main source of divine revelation and is regarded as the authorized word of God. It tells stories of God's nature, His promises, His will, and His dealings with humans. The Word helps us understand God's ways by acting as a lamp unto our feet and a light unto our path, according to Psalm 119:105. Permit me to say that you cannot go wrong with the scriptures.

3. Through Jesus Christ: The central revelation of God to humanity, according to Christianity, is Jesus Christ.

According to Colossians 1:15, Jesus is the human embodiment of God's essence and character, representing the invisible God. Believers learn about God's compassion, mercy, and salvation via the teachings, life, death, and resurrection of Jesus.

4. With Prayer and Meditation: Prayer is a way to speak and be in touch with God. It entails asking God for things as well as listening to His voice and asking for His direction. Christians are urged by Matthew 6:6 to pray in private because God, who sees in secret, will bless them in public.

5. Through the Holy Spirit: The Holy Spirit is essential to the revelation of God's truth and the equipping of believers to comprehend and carry out His will in their lives. The Spirit examines the deep mysteries of God and gives spiritual understanding to those who are receptive to receiving it, according to 1 Corinthians 2:10–12.3. As we increase in knowledge and comprehension of God, the Holy Spirit changes our hearts and minds to resemble Christ. 2 Corinthians 3:18 reiterates this: "And we all, who

with unveiled faces contemplate the Lord's glory, are being transformed into his image with ever-increasing glory, which comes from the Lord, who is the Spirit." We are led to conversion and restoration with God when the Spirit convinces us of sin. In John 16:8, Jesus declared, "When he comes, he will prove the world to be in the wrong about sin and righteousness and judgment." The Holy Spirit is essential in strengthening our bond with God and assisting us in comprehending His ways.

6. By Way of God's Qualities: God is described in the Bible as having many attributes, such as compassion, love, justice, purity, power, and loyalty. Every quality sheds light on God's nature and aids Christians in comprehending Him better. God is described as gracious and compassionate in Psalm 103:8, slow to anger, and abundant in unwavering love.

7. Through Community and Fellowship: A believer's understanding of God is frequently fostered in the context of their community and fellowship. Christians were exhorted to stay together and support one another, mainly as they watched the Day of the drawing nearby. Knowing God begins with community and friendship with other believers. Believers' regular get-togethers provide forums

for accountability, support, and spiritual development (Hebrews 10:24–25). Through conversations and shared experiences, believers polish and build each other's faith in the same way as iron sharpens iron (Proverbs 27:17). They encourage and support one another, fostering an atmosphere that allows people to flourish in their connection with God (1 Thessalonians 5:11, Ecclesiastes 4:9–12). Acts 2:42–47 describes how the early Christian community demonstrated the value of friendship by devoting themselves to group activities, including teaching, prayer, and resource sharing. They had tremendous experiences of God's presence because of their shared devotion, which helped them to comprehend God's nature and purposes better. Essentially, Christian community and fellowship offer pathways for believers to deepen their understanding of God. They have a deeper and closer interaction with God because of their shared ability to negotiate the difficulties of faith, encourage fellow believers through adversity, and embrace successes.

8. Through Surrender and Worship: Awe, devotion, and obedience to God are expressed through worship. As a form of spiritual devotion, Christians are commanded by Romans 12:1 to present themselves to God as holy, acceptable live sacrifices.

9. Through difficulties and Challenges: Believers can encounter God's power, consolation, and presence when they are going through difficulties and challenges. Walking through the valley of the shadow of death is described in Psalm 23:4, but do not dread evil since God is with us, consoling us with His rod and staff.

10. Through Transformation and Sanctification: Becoming acquainted with God entails a process of sanctification in which followers of Christ are molded into the likeness of Him. According to 2 Corinthians 3:18, the Lord's Spirit transforms this process from glory to glory.

Living by God's will as revealed in Scripture, accepting His sovereignty, and comprehending His attributes of justice, righteousness, and love are all part of knowing God. It's a path of trust, submission, and closeness to the Creator.

It must be emphasized that knowing God is not a destination with a set graduation date, but rather an endless journey. Understanding and being in the presence of God is a lifetime endeavor marked by constant learning, development, and transformation. Let's check some scriptures together.

In Philippians 3:10 (NIV), the Bible says, "I want to know Christ—yes, to know the power of his resurrection and participation in his sufferings, becoming like him in his death," This verse highlights the desire to know Christ deeply, implying that this is a continuous process rather than a one-time accomplishment. The Bible says, "This is what the Lord says: 'Let not the wise boast of their wisdom or the strong boast of their strength or the rich boast of their riches, but let the one who boasts boast about this: that they have the understanding to know me, that I am the Lord, who exercises kindness, justice, and righteousness on earth, for in these I delight,' declares the Lord." (Jeremiah 9:23–24 NIV). Understanding God is a lifelong process that includes comprehending His traits, ways, and character. The Bible says, "But continue to grow and increase in God's grace and intimacy with our Lord and Savior, Jesus Christ. May he receive all the glory both now and until the day eternity begins? Amen!" 2 Peter 3:18 (TPT). There is perpetually more to find out and uncover about Jesus Christ, as this verse emphasizes the significance of ongoing progress in understanding. The Bible says, "Come close to God and He will come close to you." (James 4:8 AMPC).

Understanding God is not limited to knowledge alone; knowing God is a constant invitation and journey in His presence. The Bible also says, " For now we are looking in a mirror that gives only a dim (blurred) reflection [of reality as in a riddle or enigma], but then [when perfection comes] we shall see in reality and face to face! Now I know in part (imperfectly), but then I shall know and understand fully and clearly, even in the same manner as I have been fully and known and understood [by God]." (1 Corinthians 13:12 AMPC).

This line highlights the eternal aspect of knowing God by implying that although our knowledge of Him is now restricted and incomplete, there will come a day when we shall thoroughly know Him as He perfectly knows us. To summarize, getting to know God is a lifetime endeavor characterized by development, closeness, and ongoing revelation. As we sincerely pursue Him, He will reveal Himself to us on an adventure that surpasses time and grows more profound by the day.

UNVEILING YOUR MASK

WORKBOOK

A 10-WEEK HEALING GUIDE TO WHOLENESS, SELF DISCOVERY AND FULFILLMENT

WORKBOOK

A 10-WEEK HEALING GUIDE TO WHOLENESS, SELF DISCOVERY AND FULFILLMENT

This workbook is written as a guide to the main book, covering the core message of how you can walk in your newly found journey and identity, offering prayers, declarations and practical activities. This guide will offer you insights into God's perspective and definition of you and help you navigate the crossroads of life's most important questions and moments of reflection on what truly matters.

Just as the main book invites you into a journey of transformation, where you discover your identity, walk in purpose and grow spiritually and intentionally, this workbook is designed to accompany you as you go deeper into the principles and practices outlined in the main book.

My life's story is a testament to the power and impact of God's Word in shaping our identity and purpose. Like you, I have experienced the confusion and frustration of searching for answers to the life's fundamental questions: Who am I? Why am I here? Where do I belong? These questions can leave you feeling adrift in a sea of uncertainty, as you desperately seek meaning and direction in life.

In the main book, I shared my personal journey of dealing with these questions and discovering life-changing truth of my identity in Christ. From childhood struggles to false identities and broken relationships, I've experienced firsthand the challenges of going through an identity crisis. But through encountering Jesus and cultivating a deep relationship with Him, I've found freedom, restoration and purpose.

This workbook is your guide to experiencing similar breakthroughs in your own life. Through reflective exercises, journaling and practical applications, you will experience healing, wholeness and transformation. This book will guide you to living fully in the freedom of Christ, as you embrace your true identity as son or daughter of the Most High.

This is a 10-week guide, with practical daily activities to engage in. As you go through this workbook, I encourage you to approach the content with openness, authenticity and vulnerability. Allow yourself to be guided by the Holy Spirit as you go into the depths of your heart and the truth of God's Word. Remember, this journey is not about acquiring knowledge, but experiencing genuine shifts in your thinking, beliefs and behaviors.

I believe that as you commit to this 20-day journey of self-discovery and spiritual growth, you will begin to experience joy, peace and fulfillment that come from walking in your true identity in Christ. So, let's get started on this journey, confident in the promise of full circle, a promise of restoration, renewal and redemption in every area of your life.

WEEK ONE

APPOINTED AND ANOINTED

Bible Reading: Jeremiah 1:5-8, Ephesians 2:10, 1 Peter 2:9-10

The passage from Jeremiah 1:5 reminds us of God's intimate involvement in our lives even before we are born. It awakens us to the realization that our identities are not merely products of chance or circumstance but are part of God's divine plan. This awakening spark a journey of self-discovery and growth, leading us to explore and walk in the light of our identity in Christ.

The foundation of our identity lies in the biblical truth that we are created in the image of God. This implies a reflection of His attributes and a unique purpose for each individual. While external factors may influence how we perceive ourselves, our true identity can only be found in Christ. In the New Testament, you will notice a recurring phrase, being "in Christ", it shows our union with Christ, beyond the usual, and shapes our understanding of our value as redeemed children of God.

Just as God knew Jeremiah before he was formed in the womb and appointed him as a prophet, He knows you, and you are uniquely appointed and anointed by God for a specific purpose. This divine calling defines your significance and worth as vessels in God's redemptive plan. Walking in your true identity is a journey of purpose. It requires you seeking God's guidance and surrendering your ambitions to His sovereign will.

Through prayer, meditation on Scripture, and wise counsel, you can uncover God's purposes for your lives and walk in obedience to His direction. The anointing of God's Spirit empowers you to fulfill your divine assignments, overcome obstacles, and make a lasting impact in the world. As vessels of His anointing, you are called to embody His love, mercy, and grace, shining as beacons of hope in a world in need of redemption.

This Week's Confession

"I am appointed and anointed
by God for a divine purpose.
I embrace my unique calling and
walk confidently in my identity in Christ.
With His guidance and empowerment,

I fulfill my destiny

and make a significant impact in the world."

Activities of the week

- Day One: Scripture Meditation
  Set aside time each day to meditate on scriptures
  that speak to the theme of being appointed and
  anointed by God. Reflect on passages such as
  Jeremiah 1:5, Isaiah 61:1-3, and 1 Peter 2:9,
  allowing their truth to sink deep into your heart and
  spirit.

- Day Two: Prayer
  Spend time in prayer, seeking God's guidance and
  wisdom regarding your appointed purpose and
  anointing. Ask Him to reveal His plan for your life
  and to empower you with His Holy Spirit to fulfill it.

- Day Three: Reflection
  Reflect on past experiences where you have seen
  God's hand at work in your life, confirming His
  calling and anointing upon you.

- Day Four: Journaling

  Keep a journal dedicated to documenting your journey of discovering and embracing your appointed purpose and anointing. Write down insights, revelations, and prayers as you seek to align yourself with God's will for your life. Use this journal as a tool for self-reflection and spiritual growth.

- Day Five: Mentorship

  Seek out mentors who can support you in discerning and fulfilling your appointed purpose and anointing. Surround yourself with wise counsel and godly encouragement, allowing others to speak into your life and help you stay focused on God's plan for you.

- Day Six: Accountability

  Surround yourself with accountability partners who are aware of who you are and are willing to journey together with you. Companions are important to help you during your weak moments.

- Day Seven: Review

Review all activities of the week and make decisions that align with your goals.

WEEK TWO

THE QUEST BEGINS

Bible Reading: Psalm 139:13-14, Ephesians 2:10, Romans 12:2

The chapter inspires a yearning to surpass the limitations of physical boundaries and time constraints, in order to intentionally seek God and discover who you truly are. The journey is likened to an odyssey, highlighting its importance and everlasting consequences.

Commencing the journey of self-discovery requires a moment of introspection; recognizing the need to delve deeper into the recesses of the heart and mind, seeking God in prayer and meditation in God's Word. This introspection catalyzes peeling back the layers of societal expectations, personal insecurities, and cultural conditioning to reveal the authentic self beneath.

The quest for self-discovery is considered vital because it arises from the human spirit's innate desire for significance, direction, and satisfaction. It goes beyond material possessions and temporary gratifications, providing a route to genuine joy and fulfillment. Additionally, it unlocks the door to one's authentic identity in Christ, urging people to live out their faith as a life-changing truth.

Furthermore, the journey empowers individuals to live authentically and purposefully, liberating them from the shackles of conformity and enabling them to embrace their unique gifts, talents, and passions. This authenticity fosters integrity, confidence, and conviction, allowing individuals to shine as beacons of light in a world shrouded in darkness.

This Week's Confession

I am on a quest for my true identity in Christ.
I embrace the journey of self-discovery with courage, curiosity, and an open heart.
Each step I take brings me closer to realizing my fullest potential and living out God's purpose for my life.
I am fearfully and wonderfully made, uniquely crafted by the hands of my Creator.
I embrace every aspect of who I am with love, acceptance, and gratitude.

I am empowered by the Holy Spirit to walk in authenticity, confidence, and purpose.

My identity is found in Christ alone, and in Him, I am complete.

Activities of the week

- Day One: Journaling
  Set aside time each day to journal about your thoughts, feelings, and experiences on the journey of self-discovery in Christ. Reflect on Scripture passages that speak to your identity in Christ and write down any insights or revelations you receive.

- Day Two: Prayer and Meditation
  Spend quiet time in prayer and meditation, seeking God's guidance and wisdom as you navigate the quest for your true identity. Ask the Holy Spirit to reveal hidden truths about yourself and to empower you to live authentically in Christ.

- Day Three: Scripture Study

Dedicate time to studying relevant Scriptures that speak to your identity in Christ, such as Ephesians 1:3-14, 2 Corinthians 5:17, and Romans 8:14-17. Reflect on how these passages inform your understanding of who you are in Christ and how they shape your perspective on self-discovery.

- Day Four: Personal Reflection
  Set aside time for personal reflection and introspection. Consider your strengths, weaknesses, passions, and values, and how they align with God's purposes for your life. Reflect on past experiences and how they have shaped your sense of identity.

- Day Five: Community Engagement
  Engage with fellow believers in discussions and activities focused on identity in Christ. Join a small group or Bible study where you can share your journey of self-discovery and glean insights from others who are also on a similar quest.

- Day Six: Seek Counsel

   Don't hesitate to seek counsel from trusted mentors, pastors, or Christian counselors who can provide guidance and support on your journey of self-discovery. Share your struggles, questions, and aspirations with them and allow their wisdom to enrich your quest.

- Day Seven: Review

   Review all activities of the week and make decisions that align with your goals.

CHAPTER 3

UNVEILING YOUR MASK

Bible Reading: Colossians 3:9-10, Ephesians 4:22-24

The passage from Ephesians 4:22-24 exhorts you to shed your old self, characterized by deceitful desires, and to embrace your new self, created in righteousness and holiness. In the pursuit of acceptance and purpose, individuals often adopt false identities, sacrificing their true selves to fit societal expectations or gain approval. However, clinging to these false identities leads to a loss of authenticity and genuine connection.

The passage calls for a radical transformation, urging individuals to discard their old selves and be renewed in the attitude of their minds. This process involves confronting the truth behind the facades, acknowledging fears, insecurities, and vulnerabilities without judgment. It requires introspection, self-reflection, and seeking guidance from trusted mentors to uncover the true self beneath the masks.

The story of the Samaritan woman at the well in John 4 illustrates the consequences of hiding behind layers of shame and societal expectations. Jesus sees beyond her past mistakes and social status, inviting her to embrace her true self and find fulfillment in authentic connection with Him. Similarly, be encouraged to lay down your masks and encounter Christ, who knows you fully and loves you unconditionally.

Navigating the balance between adapting to social contexts and remaining true to oneself starts with self-awareness and reflection. It involves integrating different aspects of oneself into a cohesive whole, embracing imperfections and limitations as integral parts of identity. Shedding masks requires vulnerability, humility, and courage, leading to a profound sense of liberation and empowerment.

This week's Confession

I am worthy of love and acceptance just as I am.
I embrace my authenticity and vulnerability,
knowing that they are my greatest strengths.
As I unveil my masks,
I walk confidently in my true identity,

shining brightly as a beacon of light in the world.

Activities of the week

- Day One: Journaling
  Set aside time each day to reflect on your thoughts, feelings, and experiences. Use journal prompts to explore the masks you wear and the aspects of your authentic self that you want to unveil. Write freely and without judgment, allowing yourself to express your true thoughts and emotions.

- Day Two: Self-Reflection
  Take a quiet moment to sit in silence and reflect on your behaviors, actions, and interactions with others. Ask yourself if you are being true to your authentic self or if you are wearing a mask to fit in or avoid conflict. Challenge yourself to identify areas where you can be more authentic and vulnerable in your relationships and interactions.

- Day Three: Mindfulness Practice

Engage in mindfulness exercises such as deep breathing or meditation, to cultivate self-awareness and presence in the moment. Notice when you are tempted to put on a mask or hide behind a facade, and gently bring your awareness back to your true self.

- Day Four: Creative Expression
  Explore your authentic self through creative expression, such as writing, painting, or music. Use art as a tool for self-discovery and self-expression, allowing yourself to tap into your deepest thoughts, emotions, and desires without inhibition.

- Day Five: Community Support
  Seek out supportive communities or groups where you can share your journey of unveiling your masks and walking in your true identity. Connect with like-minded individuals who are also on a path of self-discovery and authenticity, and offer each other encouragement, support, and accountability.

- Day Six: Seek Counsel

  Seek counsel from trusted mentors, pastors, or Christian counselors who can provide guidance and support on your journey to healing. Share your struggles, questions, and aspirations with them and allow their wisdom to guide you.

- Day Seven: Review

  Review all activities of the week and make decisions that align with your goals.

CHAPTER 4

FREEDOM FROM OFFENCE

Bible Reading: Matthew 18:21-22, Ephesians 4:31-32

Freedom from offense is a significant in the journey toward discovering and walking in our true identity in Christ. At its core, freedom from offense begins with genuine forgiveness - a process that liberates us from the shackles of bitterness, resentment, and anger. In this chapter, I shared about the multifaceted nature of offense, its origins, manifestations, and consequences in our lives.

The chapter commences with a foundational understanding of what constitutes offense. Drawing from biblical and contextual definitions, offense is identified as a perceived slight or wrongdoing that evokes feelings of resentment, anger, or hurt. This definition sets the stage for how offense can find its way into various aspects of our lives, hindering genuine relationships and impeding our growth and development.

I shared personal stories and reflections on how offense, rooted in trust issues and false identities, has affected my journey of faith. From strained relationships with authority figures to betrayal by trusted leaders, I discussed the impact of offense on their spiritual and emotional well-being. These experiences serve as reminders of the nature of offense and the need to take intentional steps toward freedom and healing.

From Ephesians 4:31-32, we see the need for forgiveness in breaking free from the bondage of offense. Through forgiveness, individuals release themselves from the grip of bitterness and resentment, opening the door to reconciliation and restoration in relationships. Also, the chapter examines the various forms and manifestations of offense, challenging you to recognize and address offense in your own lives. Whether intentional or accidental, offense can have profound consequences on your relationships and spiritual well-being.

Practical strategies for guarding against offense are rooted in biblical principles of discretion, peacemaking, and love. The book of Proverbs serves as a rich source of wisdom on communication and conflict resolution, highlighting the importance of humility and empathy when dealing with interpersonal relationships. Additionally, the power of love is a catalyst for reconciliation and healing.

This week's Confession

I am free from the bondage of offense.

Through the power of God's grace,

I release resentment, anger, and hurt,

choosing instead to walk in forgiveness, love, and reconciliation.

I guard my heart with wisdom,

pursue peace with all men,

and embody the transformative power of love in my interactions.

My identity is rooted in Christ, and

I refuse to be ensnared by the traps of offense.

I am an agent of reconciliation,

extending grace and compassion to others

as I walk in freedom and authenticity.

Activities of the week

- Day One: Reflection and Journaling
  Set aside time each day for reflection and journaling on instances where you have felt offended or have offended others. Explore the root causes of these

offenses and reflect on how you can respond with grace and forgiveness. Write down prayers of release and surrender, committing to walk in freedom from offense.

- Day Two: Scripture Meditation
  Meditate on scriptures that speak to the theme of forgiveness, love, and reconciliation. Memorize verses such as Matthew 18:21-22, Colossians 3:13, and Ephesians 4:31-32, allowing their truth to permeate your heart and mind. Use these scriptures as a source of strength and guidance in moments of offense.

- Day Three: Prayer and Intercession
  Spend time in prayer, lifting up those who have offended you and asking God for the grace to forgive and extend love. Pray for wisdom and discernment in navigating challenging relationships and intercede on behalf of those who are caught in the cycle of offense. Surrender your hurts and

grievances to God, trusting Him to bring healing and reconciliation.

- Day Four: Acts of Kindness
  Intentionally perform acts of kindness and generosity towards those who have offended you or whom you have offended. Reach out with a word of encouragement, a thoughtful gesture, or a sincere apology, seeking to mend broken relationships and restore peace. By extending grace and compassion, you demonstrate the transformative power of love in overcoming offense.

- Day Five: Community Engagement
  Engage with your faith community or small group to discuss the topic of offense and forgiveness. Share your experiences and struggles and encourage one another to walk in freedom and authenticity. Pray for one another, offering support and accountability in the journey towards healing and reconciliation.

- Day Six: Forgiveness Exercise

  Practice the discipline of forgiveness through a guided exercise. Write down the names of individuals who have offended you, along with specific incidents or grievances. As you meditate on each name, choose to release them from the debt of offense, offering forgiveness as an act of obedience to God. Tear up or burn the list as a symbolic gesture of letting go and walking in freedom.

- Day Seven: Review

  Review all activities of the week and make decisions that align with your goals.

CHAPTER 5

WALKING IN FORGIVENESS

Bible Reading: Matthew 6:14-15, Ephesians 4:31-32, Matthew 18:21-22

In the journey of walking in your true identity, forgiveness plays an important role in releasing you from the shackles and allowing you to walk authentically in your true self. In this chapter, I spoke about the power of forgiveness and its significance in our quest for authenticity.

As Jesus teaches, forgiveness knows no limit. It is not a one-time action but a continuous practice that requires consistent effort. Jesus exemplified this by emphasizing forgiveness in His teachings and incorporating it into the model prayer He shared with His disciples. The command to forgive extends beyond human limitations, reflecting God's boundless mercy and grace.

What is forgiveness? It is the act of releasing and remitting, a gift you give yourself rather than exonerating the perpetrator. Forgiveness liberates you and frees you from the bondage of bitterness and resentment. The parable of the unmerciful servant illustrates the essence of forgiveness; showing mercy and letting go of offenses, reflecting God's forgiveness towards humanity (Matthew 18:21-35).

Living in forgiveness is not without its challenges. It requires obedience and a conscious decision to let go of grudges and resentment. While forgiveness may seem daunting, it is a commandment, not a suggestion. Through forgiveness, we maintain purity of heart, prevent resentment from taking root, and experience healing and restoration.

The Holy Spirit serves as our guide and helper in the journey of forgiveness. By yielding to His control, we receive the strength and willingness to forgive, even in the face of adversity. Obedience to God's Word is paramount in walking in forgiveness, as it transforms our perspectives and empowers us to extend grace and mercy to others.

This week's Confession

I embrace the high calling of walking in forgiveness.

Forgiveness knows no limits, and I choose

to extend grace and mercy seventy times seven.

As I release resentment and bitterness,

I discover freedom and healing.

I choose to see the good in every offense,

embracing opportunities for personal growth,

empathy, and reconciliation.

My heart is filled with compassion, kindness, and love,

reflecting the forgiveness I have received from my Heavenly Father.

Activities of the week

- Day One: Daily Forgiveness Practice

  Set aside time each day for a forgiveness practice. Begin by quieting your heart and mind through prayer and meditation. Reflect on any offenses or grievances you may be holding onto, both towards yourself and others. Choose to release these burdens through forgiveness, speaking words of grace and mercy over yourself and those who have wronged you. Visualize letting go of these hurts and embracing freedom and healing.

- Day Two: Scripture Reflection

  Meditate on scriptures that speak to the theme of forgiveness, such as Matthew 18:21-22, Colossians 3:13, and Ephesians 4:31-32. Take time to journal your thoughts and reflections on these verses, noting how they apply to your own journey of forgiveness. Allow God's Word to penetrate your heart and mind, guiding you in the practice of walking in forgiveness.

- Day Three: Letter of Forgiveness

  Write a letter of forgiveness to someone who has hurt you in the past. Pour out your thoughts and emotions on paper, expressing your decision to release them from the debt of offense. Be honest and vulnerable in your letter, acknowledging the pain caused but choosing to extend grace and mercy. You may choose to send the letter or keep it for your own healing process.

- Day Four: Acts of Kindness

  Engage in acts of kindness towards those you have forgiven or those who have wronged you. Look for opportunities to show love and compassion, extending grace in practical ways. Whether it's a kind word, a thoughtful gesture, or a simple act of service, let your actions reflect the forgiveness and healing you have experienced.

- Day Five: Prayer for Healing

  Spend time in prayer, inviting God to heal any wounds or hurts that linger from past offenses. Surrender these hurts to Him, asking for His grace and mercy to bring healing and restoration. Pray for the strength to continue walking in forgiveness, trusting in God's faithfulness to guide you on this journey.

- Day Six: Community Support

  Seek support and accountability from your faith community or a trusted friend. Share your struggles and victories in the journey of forgiveness and ask for prayer and encouragement. Surround yourself with people who will uplift and support you as you continue to walk in forgiveness and healing.

- Day Seven: Review
Review all activities of the week and make decisions that align with your goals.

CHAPTER 6

MANAGING REJECTION

Bible Reading: Romans 8:35-39, 1 Peter 2:4-5, Psalm 27:10,

Rejection is a universal experience that touches the lives of individuals across races, ethnicity, and continents. It is often accompanied by feelings of inadequacy, shame, and despair, challenging our sense of worth and purpose. However, rejection was never part of God's original design for humanity. It entered our lives as a result of sin, disrupting our relationships and distorting our identities.

Throughout history, rejection has played a prominent role in human relationships, from Adam and Eve's rejection of God to Peter's denial of Jesus. The pain of rejection is deeply felt whether it's the rejection of a romantic partner, a friend, or even a family member. Rejection can leave you feeling isolated, hurt, and questioning your value.

The story of Joseph in the Book of Genesis provides a powerful example of how rejection can ultimately lead to God's favor and redemption. Despite being sold into slavery by his own brothers, Joseph remained faithful to God, recognizing that what others meant for harm, God intended for good. Similarly, Jesus himself experienced rejection during his earthly ministry but ultimately brought salvation to the world through his sacrificial love.

Understanding the effects of rejection is crucial for managing its impact on our lives. Rejection can manifest in various forms, including loneliness, self-pity, depression, and even thoughts of suicide. It can harden your hearts, breed indifference, and lead to rebellion or involvement in harmful practices like witchcraft. However, you are called to lean on your belief in God's plan for your life and trust that He is close to the brokenhearted, offering comfort and strength in your times of need.

In managing rejection, it is essential to embrace your identity in Christ and follow His example of humility, grace, and love. You can learn from biblical examples like Joseph, who remained faithful to God despite experiencing rejection and betrayal. Seeking wisdom, cultivating mercy and truth, and building healthy relationships with authority figures are also essential aspects of managing rejection effectively.

Rejection does not define us. Our worth and identity are found in Christ, not in the opinions or actions of others. Through prayer, reliance on God's word, and trust in His plan for our lives, we can overcome the pain of rejection and emerge stronger, more resilient, and fully rooted in our true identity as beloved children of God.

This Week's Confession

I am worthy and valued,

not defined by rejection but by the love and favor of God.

I embrace my identity in Christ,

knowing that His grace sustains me, and His favor surrounds me.

I am empowered to overcome rejection.

with resilience, wisdom, and love.

Each day, I grow stronger, more confident,

and more rooted in the truth of who I am in Him.

Activities of the week

- Day One: Reflective Journaling
  Set aside time each day to reflect on your thoughts and emotions regarding rejection. Write down any

instances of rejection you've experienced and how they made you feel. Then, counteract those negative thoughts with declarations of your worth in Christ and reminders of His unfailing love for you.

- Day Two: Prayer and Meditation
Spend time in prayer and meditation, seeking God's presence and guidance in overcoming rejection. Ask Him to fill you with His peace and assurance, knowing that you are fearfully and wonderfully made in His image.

- Day Three: Scripture Study
Explore into Scripture and study passages that speak to God's favor and love for His children. Highlight verses that remind you of your identity in Christ and His promises of blessing and provision. Meditate on these verses daily to renew your mind and strengthen your faith.

- Day Four: Acts of Kindness

Engage in acts of kindness and service towards others, focusing on showing love and compassion to those who may be experiencing rejection or hardship themselves. By extending grace and love to others, you'll also experience the healing power of God's love in your own life.

- Day Five: Positive Declarations
  Create personalized declarations based on Scripture and God's promises. Repeat these declarations daily, speaking to them aloud with confidence and conviction. Declarations such as "I am loved and accepted by God," "I am chosen and valued," and "I am fearfully and wonderfully made" can help reinforce your identity in Christ and combat feelings of rejection.

- Day Six: Community Support
  Surround yourself with a supportive community of fellow believers who can uplift and encourage you in your journey. Share your struggles and victories with trusted friends or a mentor who can offer guidance and prayer support.

- Day Seven: Review

  Review all activities of the week and make decisions that align with your goals.

CHAPTER 7

DELIVERANCE

In the journey of walking in our true identity in Christ, one essential aspect is deliverance. Deliverance, in a spiritual sense, refers to being freed from bondage, oppression, and captivity by the power of God. It encompasses liberation from spiritual strongholds, emotional burdens, addictions, generational curses, and demonic influences. In this chapter, I shared the significance of deliverance in walking in our true identity and the transformative power it brings to our lives.

It started with an emphasis on the foundational deliverance found in salvation. Through Christ, believers are rescued from the dominion of darkness and brought into the kingdom of light. This liberation from darkness symbolizes freedom from confusion, shame, and false identities, allowing individuals to embrace their authentic selves in Christ.

Deliverance is portrayed as a process of moving from a state of sin, negativity, or devastation into one of safety, strength, and spiritual healing. It involves fervent prayer, faith, and reliance on God's power to rescue us from adversity and evil. Throughout the Bible, God is portrayed as the ultimate deliverer, offering freedom and restoration to His people in times of need.

Also, I shared about God's promises of deliverance from various forms of bondage, including addiction, fear, unbelief, illness, and demonic oppression. I highlight biblical examples such as the deliverance of the Israelites from Egypt and Jesus' ministry of healing and liberation during His time on earth.

Furthermore, the concept of "children's bread" is introduced, emphasizing that deliverance is a privilege for believers. Just as physical bread nourishes the body, deliverance nourishes the soul, providing healing, restoration, and freedom to God's children. This is about God's abundant grace and provision for His people.

In this chapter. I talked about the importance of breaking free from the grip of the past and toxic relationships. Through Christ, you can experience healing from past wounds, forgiveness for past offenses, and freedom from unhealthy relational dynamics. When you surrender to

God's transformative work, you can embrace a future of wholeness and purpose in alignment with God's divine plan.

This week's Confession

I am a child of God,

and His promise of healing and deliverance is my birthright.

I embrace freedom from the past,

release toxic relationships,

and step into the purpose and wholeness that God has destined for me.

With faith and courage,

I walk in the transformative power of His grace,

knowing that His plans for me are good,

filled with hope and a future.

Activities for the week

- Day One: Reflective Journaling
  Take some time each day to reflect on your past experiences, acknowledging any wounds or hurts that may still be affecting you. Write about how these experiences have impacted your life and

relationships and express your desire for healing
and deliverance.

- Day Two: Prayer and Meditation
  Spend time in prayer and meditation, seeking God's
  guidance and wisdom in the journey of healing and
  deliverance. Ask Him to reveal any areas of your
  life where you need His healing touch and surrender
  those areas to Him in faith.

- Day Three: Forgiveness Practice
  Practice forgiveness towards yourself and others,
  releasing any bitterness or resentment that may be
  holding you back. Write a letter of forgiveness to
  anyone who has hurt you, expressing your decision
  to let go of the past and move forward in freedom.

- Day Four: Healthy Boundaries
  Evaluate your relationships and set healthy
  boundaries with those who may be toxic or
  unhealthy for you. Identify any patterns of behavior

that need to change and commit to prioritizing your emotional and spiritual well-being.

- Day Five: Seeking Purpose
  Spend time seeking God's purpose for your life, asking Him to reveal His plans and dreams for you. Write down any insights or inspirations that come to mind and take practical steps towards fulfilling God's calling on your life.

- Day Six: Community Support
  Surround yourself with a supportive community of believers who can encourage and uplift you on your journey of healing and deliverance. Seek out a mentor or counsellor who can provide guidance and accountability as you pursue wholeness in Christ.

- Day Seven: Review
  Review all activities of the week and make decisions that align with your goals.

CHAPTER 8

WALKING IN FAITH

Bible Reading: James 2:14-26, Mark 9:14-29, Matthew 14:22-33

In this chapter, I deeply shared the concept of faith as an essential aspect of the Christian journey. I defined faith and its importance in the believer's life and provided practical insights on how to cultivate and live out a life of faith.

I emphasized the significance of faith as a foundational element of the Christian identity. Drawing from Hebrews 11:1, the chapter establishes faith as the assurance of things hoped for and the conviction of things not seen. Faith is the guiding belief system that enables believers to unlock their potential and achieve remarkable feats by trusting in God's promises.

Faith is more than just a fleeting sentiment, but a steadfast conviction rooted in the eternal truths of Scripture. Faith is not merely a passive acknowledgment, but an active confidence based on the unseen truths of God's promises. Moreover, I shared various biblical examples of individuals who exemplified unwavering faith in the face of adversity. From Moses' encounter with the burning bush to Peter's declaration of Jesus as the Messiah, these stories serve as timeless reminders of the power of faith and how mere people can become powerful heroes of faith.

Walking in faith is a continuous journey rather than a one-time occurrence. Be encouraged to trust in God's guidance even when the path ahead is unclear and to hold fast to your faith in the face of difficulties and setbacks.

Declarations

I trust in God's promises,
knowing that He is faithful to fulfill them.
I walk by faith, not by sight,
trusting in God's guidance even when the path ahead is unclear.
My faith in God gives me strength.
to overcome obstacles and face challenges with courage.
I believe that God is with me always,
leading me into a future filled with hope and promise.
I surrender my worries and fears to God,

knowing that He cares for me and will never leave me.

I am confident in God's plan for my life,

trusting that He will work all things together for my good.

I choose to walk in faith every day,

knowing that God's love and grace are sufficient for me.

Activities of the week

- Day One: Daily Prayer and Meditation
  Set aside time each day to pray and meditate on God's word, seeking His guidance and strength to walk in faith.

- Day Two: Study Scripture
  Go deeper into the Bible to understand God's promises and develop a firm foundation of faith.

- Day Three: Journaling
  Keep a faith journal to record your prayers, thoughts, and experiences of God's faithfulness in your life.

- Day Four: Fellowship with Believers

Surround yourself with fellow believers who can encourage and support you on your journey of faith.

- Day Five: Step Out in Faith
  Take bold steps of faith by stepping out of your comfort zone and trusting God to lead you.

- Day Six: Serve Others
  Look for opportunities to serve others in your community, demonstrating your faith through acts of love and kindness.

- Day Seven: Review
  Review all activities of the week and make decisions that align with your goals.

CHAPTER 9

WALKING IN LOVE

Bible Reading: 1 John 4:19-21, John 13:34-35, John 4:7-8

Walking in love lies at the heart of the Christian faith, reflecting God's compassion and care for others. Love is not merely a feeling, but a conscious choice demonstrated through actions and attitudes. In this chapter, we learned the essence of love as a foundational commandment for believers, and emphasized its power and significance in the Christian journey and those we journey with.

Love is a commandment from God: love God with all our being and love our neighbors as ourselves (Mark 12:30-31). Love is more than a fleeting emotion but a steadfast, sacrificial, and constant attribute of God's nature, demonstrated through His ultimate act of love in sending His Son for humanity (John 3:16).

A passage from 1 Corinthians 13:4-8 outlines the characteristics of love, emphasizing its patient, kind, and selfless nature. Love transcends boundaries and encompasses everyone, reflecting God's boundless love for all humanity, even those considered adversaries (Matthew 5:43-48).

Walking in love entails embodying Christ's mercy and compassion in our interactions with others, extending practical acts of kindness, justice, and grace. By doing these, we express our authentic self. However, various obstacles such as pride, selfishness, and unresolved conflicts can hinder our ability to love unconditionally. Through God's love, we can overcome these challenges and extend grace and forgiveness to one another (Ephesians 4:32). To walk in your true identity, you must be intentional about walking in love. True unconditional love can change the world, one heart at a time.

This week's Confession

I am called to walk in love,
reflecting the boundless love of God in my life.
Love is my identity and my purpose, and
I embrace the opportunity to extend grace,
compassion, and kindness to those around me.
With each step I take in love,
I embody the essence of Christ and

shine His light into the world.

Activities of the week

- Day One: Random Acts of Kindness
  Challenge yourself to perform at least one random act of kindness each day. Whether it's paying for someone's coffee, complimenting a stranger, or offering a helping hand to a neighbor, these small gestures can profoundly impact others and spread love in your community.

- Day Two: Forgiveness Practice
  Take time to reflect on any past hurts or grievances you may be holding onto. Practice forgiveness towards yourself and others, releasing any bitterness or resentment that may be hindering your ability to walk in love fully.

- Day Three: Empathy Exercise
  Put yourself in someone else's shoes and try to see the world from their perspective. Practice active

listening and empathetic communication, seeking to understand their feelings and experiences without judgment or criticism.

- Day Four: Volunteer Work
Get involved in volunteer opportunities in your community or church where you can serve others and meet the needs of those less fortunate. Whether it's serving at a soup kitchen, volunteering at a homeless shelter, or participating in a mission trip, these acts of service allow you to demonstrate love in tangible ways.

- Day Five: Daily Devotional
Start each day with a devotion focused on the theme of love. Reflect on Bible verses highlighting God's love for you and His call to love others. Journal how to apply these truths daily and ask God to help you walk in love each day.

- Day Six: Accountability Partner

Find a trusted friend or mentor who can hold you accountable in your journey of walking in love. Share your struggles and victories with them and ask for prayer and support as you seek to embody God's love in your relationships and interactions.

- Day Seven: Review
  Review all activities of the week and make decisions that align with your goals.

CHAPTER 10

KNOWING GOD

Bible Reading: Jeremiah 9:23–24, Colossians 1:15, 19, Philippians 3:10

The journey of discovering and deepening our relationship with God. Drawing inspiration from the Apostle Paul's earnest desire to know Christ intimately, the chapter is about the limitless depth of fellowship and communion available to believers.

I want to emphasize that knowing God is not just about intellectual comprehension or theoretical understanding. It's an experiential process that requires a living relationship with the Creator. This relationship involves experiential knowledge, spiritual intimacy, and communion. Just like Paul, who yearned for a deeper connection with Christ, you are also called to go on a lifelong journey of discovery, continuously seeking to know God more fully.

There are various avenues through which you can deepen your understanding of God. You are invited to engage with God through prayer, meditation, and contemplation.

Through the lens of Jesus Christ, who embodies the essence of God, you can gain insight into His divine nature and character. Also, in the chapter. I highlighted the indispensable role of the Holy Spirit in guiding you to know God's truth and give you a deeper understanding of His ways. Through surrender, worship, and community fellowship, you can cultivate a conducive environment for spiritual growth and transformation.

Knowing God is not one-time, but a dynamic journey characterized by continuous learning, development, and revelation. As you earnestly pursue God, He unveils Himself in increasingly profound ways, drawing you into an ever-deepening relationship that is marked by intimacy and closeness.

This week's Confession

I am on a journey of knowing God deeply and intimately.
My heart's desire is to experience the power of His resurrection,
to share in His sufferings, and to become more like Him each day.
As I seek to know Him, I open myself to His revelation,

His presence, and His transforming love.

I embrace the lifelong adventure of growing in grace

and intimacy with my Lord and Savior, Jesus Christ.

My journey of knowing God is not limited by time or circumstance;

it is an eternal pursuit that brings joy, fulfillment,

and a profound sense of purpose to my life.

Activities for the week

- Day One: Reflective Journaling
  Set aside time each day to journal about your experiences and reflections on your journey of knowing God. Write about moments of revelation, encounters with His presence, and insights gained from studying Scripture or prayer. Reflect on how your understanding of God is evolving and deepening over time.

- Day Two: Prayer and Meditation
  Spend intentional prayer and meditation to draw closer to God and experience His presence in your

life. Use passages of Scripture, such as Psalm 139 or John 15, as prompts for meditation, allowing God to speak to your heart and reveal Himself to you in new ways.

- Day Three: Scripture Study
  Dive deeper into the Word of God, exploring passages that reveal His character, His promises, and His will for your life. Consider using resources like commentaries, devotionals, or study guides to gain a deeper understanding of Scripture and how it applies to your journey of knowing God.

- Day Four: Community and Fellowship
  Engage in meaningful relationships with other believers who are also on a journey of knowing God. Join a small group, Bible study, or prayer group where you can share your experiences, insights, and struggles with fellow travelers on the faith journey. Encourage one another, pray for one another, and hold each other accountable in your pursuit of knowing God.

- Day Five: Practicing Presence

  Cultivate a lifestyle of practicing God's presence throughout your day. Practice mindfulness and awareness of God's nearness in every moment, whether you're engaged in daily tasks, spending time with loved ones, or facing challenges. Invite God into every aspect of your life, acknowledging His presence and seeking His guidance and peace.

- Day Six: Celebrating Progress

Celebrate the progress you make on your journey of knowing God, no matter how small or incremental it may seem. Recognize and acknowledge the ways in which God is revealing Himself to you and transforming your heart and mind to be more like His. Take time to thank God for His faithfulness and provision along the way, knowing that He is always with you, guiding you into deeper intimacy with Him.

- Day Seven: Review

Review all activities of the week and make
decisions that align with your goals.

Made in the USA
Columbia, SC
30 March 2025

55894049R00112